HENRI DUPRÉ: *PURCELL*

MUSIC & MUSICIANS

BEETHOVEN: *HIS SPIRITUAL DEVELOPMENT*
By J. W. N. Sullivan

CHOPIN
By Henri Bidou

CORRESPONDENCE BETWEEN
RICHARD STRAUSS & HUGO VON HOFMANNSTHAL
1907–1918

THIRTY YEARS' MUSICAL RECOLLECTIONS
By Henry F. Chorley

MY MUSICAL LIFE
By Nikolai A. Rimsky-Korsakoff

THE WELL-TEMPERED MUSICIAN
By F. Toye

RED: *PAPERS ON MUSICAL SUBJECTS*
By Carl Van Vechten

THE WAGNERIAN ROMANCES
By Gertrude Hall

THE MUSIC OF THE PAST
By Wanda Landowska

By Ernest Newman
THE UNCONSCIOUS BEETHOVEN
WAGNER AS MAN AND ARTIST
A MUSICAL CRITIC'S HOLIDAY
A MUSICAL MOTLEY

HENRY PURCELL, *by Clostermann*

HENRI DUPRÉ
PURCELL

Translated from the French by
CATHERINE ALISON PHILLIPS
AND
AGNES BEDFORD

MCMXXVIII
ALFRED·A·KNOPF·NEW YORK

Original title

Purcell

Copyright 1927 by

Librairie Félix Alcan,

Paris

PREFACE

*T*HE NAME AND WORK OF HENRY PURCELL ARE *known to writers upon music, composers, and organists both in and out of England. This book, then, is intended for musical amateurs desirous of widening the range of their knowledge. We* *shall therefore be excused if we define certain musical terms familiar to professionals.*

How many times, in those drawing-rooms where the art of conversation still survives, have we been asked whether there is such a thing as English music! We hope that the present work may supply an answer to this question.

We have not thought it fitting to isolate Purcell from his period and surroundings. The slight historical survey and the few remarks of a literary order that the reader will find in this book have as their object to throw the figure of the English musician into relief.

We offer our sincere acknowledgments to the French and other learned writers whose names are referred to in the course of this study; and it is at once a duty and a pleasure to tender our thanks to Monsieur A. Pratz, organist of the church of Saint-Roch, Paris, whose wide experi-

ence and musical erudition have more than once guided our researches into profitable channels.

Frequent references are made to the edition of the composer's works published by the Purcell Society (referred to as P. S. Ed.), which we recommend our readers to consult. If no precise references are given to certain of Purcell's works (for example, King Arthur), the reason is that they have not yet appeared in this edition.

It is our hope that this study may succeed not only in making Henry Purcell better known, but in causing him to be loved as he deserves.

TRANSLATOR'S NOTE

The most cordial thanks are due to the LIBRARY COMMITTEE OF THE ROYAL ACADEMY OF MUSIC, LONDON, *for kindly giving permission for two photographs to be specially taken from their autograph manuscript of Purcell's* "Fairy Queen," *and in particular to* MR. WILLIAM WALLACE *for his advice, and* MR. A. HUMPHREY KEMPE, *Assistant Secretary, and President of the Purcell Opera Society, for his good offices in the matter.*

Thanks are also due to MR. LAWRENCE TANNER, *Keeper of the Muniments, and to* CANON NIXON, *Precentor and Librarian of Westminster Abbey, for their valuable assistance, and to the* STAFF OF THE BRITISH MUSEUM, *for their unfailing kindness and courtesy in facilitating the procuring of illustrations; also to* MESSRS. HEUGEL, *and in particular to* MONSIEUR BERTRAND, *for kind permission to reproduce the three musical citations on pp. 102, 106, and 121 from* Purcell: Melodies, suivies d'un duo, avec préface par Henri Dupré.

TABLE *of* CONTENTS

xi

LIST *of* ILLUSTRATIONS

xiii

HENRY PURCELL

I

English Music before Henry Purcell

THE PERIOD OF ENGLISH HISTORY DURING which Henry Purcell lived, opening with the accession of King Charles II and lasting from the year 1660 till the end of the seventeenth century, is regarded by many as the golden age of English music. Auspicious conditions led up to it and ushered it in, and it was the culminating point of a long process of evolution, the successive stages of which are marked by names that are famous, or deserve to be so, even outside England. Hence it is no phenomenon of spontaneous generation.

Were we to treat of the subject of this study without bringing him into relation with the past — were we to keep Purcell strictly isolated within the limits of his period — the reader would be unable to form a just estimate of the place that he occupies in musical history. For this reason, before approaching the subject of Purcell's life it seems to us absolutely necessary in the first place to give some account of the atmosphere in which his musical ancestors passed their lives, and next to define the general character of their art, in order to show in what respects our composer resembles and differs from them.

From the beginning of the sixteenth century, and throughout its whole course, musicians received encouragement, whether directly or indirectly, from the kings and queens of England, who were one and all ardent students of music. The virginal, the ancestor of the harpsichord, was then in high favour. Elizabeth of York, wife of Henry VII, Catherine of Aragon and Anne Boleyn, wives of Henry VIII, Henry VIII himself, Edward VI, Mary Tudor, and Queen Elizabeth were all accomplished executants; and

4

FACSIMILE OF A MS. OF THE KING'S BALLAD

Henry VIII was a composer. Both music written for keyboard instruments and choral music developed under their influence. In the seventeenth century James I founded the Musicians' Company of London by letters patent. Charles I, whose taste is said by Macaulay to have been excellent, was careful to indicate in person what anthems were to be sung at divine service, and was ready to play his part on the viol da gamba in the Fantasias of Coperario, *alias* Cooper. This Cooper, an Englishman by birth, had thought fit to Italianize his name during his residence in Italy. In 1636 Charles I reorganized the Musicians' Company, and himself appointed Laniere as its head with the title of Marshal. This Laniere could claim the merit of introducing the *stilo recitativo* (the new Italian style of accompanied recitative) into English music.

Abundant details illustrating the intensity of musical life in the time of Charles I will be found in Shorthouse's novel *John Inglesant*.

With regard to the way in which sacred music was interpreted at the court of Henry VIII we have the testimony of the Venetian ambassador. " Mass was sung," he writes, " by His Majesty's choristers. Their voices are divine rather than human. They did not sing after the fashion of men, but praised God after the manner of angels. I do not think the bass voices have their equal anywhere in the world."

Shakspere, as is well known, was passionately devoted to music. His style is scattered with allusions to musical technique, so much so that an English writer, Edward W. Naylor, has written quite a substantial work, *Shakespeare and Music*, on the subject of the relations of the poet to the Muse of harmony and lyric poetry.

Thomas Tusser recommended mistresses to choose servants who were fond of music. In his *A hundrethe Good Points of Husbandrie lately married unto a Hundrethe Good Points of Huswifry* (1570), which MM. E. Legouis and L. Cazamian, in their *Histoire de la littérature anglaise,* characterize as a compendium of " practical wisdom, utterly commonplace, but lacking in neither animation nor humour," we find the following distich:

> Such servants are oftenest painful and good
> That sing in their labour as birds in the wood.

Thomas Morley, in *A Plaine and Easie Introduction to Practicall Musicke* (1597), alludes to the astonishment displayed by cultivated people when Philomathes showed himself incapable of reading his part in a chorus at sight. " How can he have been brought up? " whispered those around him. Nobody could claim to be a man of the world if he had not studied music.

Peacham, in his *Compleat Gentleman*, declares that no wise man has ever called in question the legitimacy of the practice of music, the sister of poetry. " Music," he adds, " is a gift of Heaven, granted to man that he may praise and extol his Creator, and to console him for the cares and griefs with which life is assailed at every hour." Then follow some considerations with regard to the practical utility of music, which, according to the physicians, prolongs life, cures certain diseases, is an antidote to the bite of the tarantula, corrects defects of pronunciation, and is a remedy for stammering in children.

According to Sir John Hawkins (1719–89), the author of a history of music, the Statutes of Trinity College, Cambridge, made it obligatory upon candidates for fellowships to be able to sing. Hawkins's assertion is somewhat exaggerated. Naylor, Aldis Wright, and the Rev. H. F. Stewart confine themselves to stating that skill in the art of song conferred an advantage upon a candidate in case of equality with another.

The madrigal, of Flemish origin, continued to be very fashionable in the second half of the sixteenth century and up to the third decade of the seventeenth.

The masque was very much in vogue at the court of James I and his successor Charles I. It was a dramatic entertainment, the subject of which was generally allegorical or mythological, and in which poetry, vocal and instrumental music, dancing, and stage-craft combined to delight the eyes and ears. The best poets of the day, Ben Jonson, Beaumont and Fletcher, Heywood, Thomas Carew, and, last but not least, Milton himself, were addicted to this style of literature and art. The famous architect Inigo Jones was called in, as Brunelleschi or Leonardo da Vinci had formerly been in the *Sacre Rappresentazioni,* to arrange the details of the stage setting and to design decorations and costumes. The musicians of the period, Laniere, Lawes, and, later on, Christopher Gibbons and Lock, provided the music. The masque was the precursor of opera.

The taste for music gradually spread abroad among the masses. Cobblers, tin-smiths, tinkers, and coal-heavers amused themselves by singing " catches," a sort of composition for several voices, most usually in the form of a canon. We have evidence of this in various dramatic works of the period, in Edwardes's *Damon and Pithias* (1565?), Peele's *Old Wives' Tale* (1595), Beaumont and Fletcher's *The Coxcomb* and *Bonduca*. In *Bonduca* the Roman soldiers sing a catch in three parts, an anachronism valuable for the light that it throws upon the habits of the people at the time. Naylor also quotes Samuel Harsnet's *Declaration of Egregious Impostures* (1603), in which some tinkers are represented as sitting round the fire enjoying the music of a catch, with a pot of beer between their legs. Catches were to the common people what madrigals were to the cultivated classes. Another example of the interest in music shown by the lower orders is to be found in Cyril Tourneur's *Atheist's Tragedy* (1611), in which Cataplasma, an old-clothes-woman, gives a lesson on the lute to her servant Soquette.

The taste of the English people for music was in full course of development when the Revolution broke out; so that it was in an atmosphere favourable to the production and development of musical ability that such masters flourished as Tallis, born in the second decade of the sixteenth century, who is regarded as the father of the new religious music known as " Cathedral

music "; Christopher Tye, who in 1553 set to
music the first fourteen chapters of the Acts of
the Apostles, and is distinguished for the virile
qualities of his style; William Byrd (1538–1623),
who gives proof of great elevation of thought in
his sacred compositions, and displays certain
strikingly picturesque qualities in his pieces written for the virginal, which are directly inspired
by a feeling for nature, and to which Rubinstein
in his day, and more recently Madame Wanda
Landowska, have taken pleasure in doing justice;
Thomas Weelkes, the author of delightful madrigals, whom our contemporary Gustav Holst sa-
luted as his musical ancestor at a meeting of the
Madrigal Society of Kingston-on-Thames on November 3, 1923; John Bull (1563–1628), who has
left pieces for the virginal full of life and colour;
and Orlando Gibbons, known as the English
Palestrina, in whom nobility of inspiration and
purity of writing were combined. Around these
great names are grouped a multitude of names of
composers of lesser renown, whose works are
none the less worthy of the attention of the
musical historian, and bear witness to the artistic
vitality of the period extending from the reign
of Henry VII to the Revolution of 1640. To the
names of Laniere, Lawes, and Coperario, already

mentioned, we may add those of Tomkins, Deering, and Dowland. With the exception, to some extent, of the masques, the works of the above-mentioned musicians are written in the polyphonic style, in which the melody, instead of standing out against a harmonic background, is equally distributed among all the voices. The masters of the sixteenth century depended for the interpretation of their artistic dreams upon choirs.

Polyphony, as M. Vincent d'Indy has shown in his *Cours de composition musicale,* was the off-spring of diaphony, or two-part harmony in its earliest form, and the descant, or ornamental counterpoint sung in combination with plain-chant, and arose from thematic imitation: the themes were heard in a series of successive " entries " and developed their melodic line horizontally, each part parallel with the other, up to the end of the chorus. The parts built themselves up, one above the other. This conception of musical composition gave rise to the fugue. It was based upon the impersonal character of the artist as an individual, and implied a complete solidarity between those singing the various parts.

Stringed instruments were subject to the same rules as voices. Thus the Fantasias of

Coperario, and the pieces for five or six viols of Deering, Dowland, Tomkins, and their like, were written according to the severest principles of polyphony. However interesting they may be to the historian of music, they lack variety. They are monotonous, owing to their predominantly scholastic character, the invariable employment of the same inevitable devices, and the narrow range of the tessitura.

The ideas of the Renaissance, which were favourable to individualism, found their way into the domain of music.

There was a revolt against the tyranny of the choir, a movement that started in Italy. Vincenzo Galilei, the father of the great astronomer, declared that the voice ought to sing *alone,* and practised what he preached by writing a musical setting for the episode of the death of Ugolino. A short time after the death of Palestrina (1594), Caccini, Peri, Emilio del Cavalieri, Viadana, guests of the Count Giovanni Bardi de Vernio at Florence, had recourse to the solo for the exposition of dramatic situations or the expression of sentiment. The monodic style was now an established fact.[1] From this new state of

[1] We employ the terms "monody" and "monodic" only in order to conform to ordinary usage. As a mat-

Come againe: sweet loue doth now enuite, thy graces that refraine, to do me due de- light, to fee, to heare, to touch, to kiffe, to die, with thee againe in fweeteft fimpha- thy.

1
Come againe that I may ceafe to mourne,
Through thy vnkind difdaine,
For now left and forlorne:
I fit, I figh, I weepe, I faind, I die,
In deadly paine, and endles miferie.

2
All the day the fun that lends me fhine,
By frownes do caufe me pine,
And feeds me with delay:
Her fmiles, my fprings, that makes my ioies to (grow,
Her frowes the winters of my woe:

All the night, my fleepes are full of dreames,
My eies are full of ftreames.

My hart takes no delight:
To fee the fruits and ioies that fome do find,
And marke the ftormes are me afignd.

3
Out alas, my faith is euer true,
Yet will fhe neuer rue,
Nor yeeld me any grace:
Her eies of fire, her hart of flint is made,
Whom teares nor truth may once inuade.

4
Gentle loue draw forth thy wounding dart,
Thou canft not pearce her hart.
For I that do approue:　　　　(fhafts
By fighs and teares more hote then are thy
Did tempt while fhe for triumps laughs.

FACSIMILE OF A PAGE FROM DOWLAND'S
First Booke of Songes and Ayres

affairs was to spring opera. Choral music, which had hitherto been the sole interpreter of religious sentiment, saw its monopoly attacked and its privileged position infringed. With the introduction of the solo, sacred music assumed a secular character, which became more accentuated every day. M. Jean Chantavoine, in his *De Couperin à Debussy* (p. 52), justly points out that architecture, sculpture, and painting in like manner assumed a somewhat worldly tinge in the course of the seventeenth century.

It now became necessary to harmonize the melody. A *basso continuo* (thorough-bass) was called in to support melodies, just as it had previously been for recitatives, and was supplemented by figures representing the intervals forming the chords struck by the accompanist. Composition, which had been horizontal, now became vertical. Throughout the whole of the sixteenth century choral singing was *a cappella* — that is, without accompaniment. If instruments were added in certain cases, they did no more than double the vocal parts. In monodic music wind or stringed instruments were called

---

ter of fact, these terms ought to apply only to *unaccompanied* melody.

into requisition to accompany the melody; in church this function had to be discharged by the organ. It appears that Viadana was responsible for this new use of the organ.

The madrigal, with which the names of Richard Edwardes, Morley, Byrd, Weelkes, Dowland, and Orlando Gibbons are for ever associated, remained faithful to the ecclesiastical — that is to say, polyphonic — style, although the words were secular and often gay. The madrigal was sung *a cappella*.

It was by way of the masque that monody made its way into England.

These few details concerning the evolution of music, which we have felt it necessary to give, are intended to make it easier to understand the struggle that was to rage between the polyphonic and monodic styles, notably in the time of Charles II.

At the period of the Reformation numbers of melodies belonging to the Roman liturgy were thrown on to the scrap-heap, but religious music did not perish. Under the sovereigns who succeeded Henry VIII up to the time of the Civil War it changed its character, adapting itself to circumstances without ceasing to be polyphonic.

During the struggle between the opposing

parties of Cavaliers and Roundheads, which ended in the beheading of Charles I, music was reduced to silence. The Puritans cast the dense shadow of their gloomily austere doctrines over English society and furiously attacked everything that might cast a gleam of beauty upon human life, and chiefly upon religious life as conceived by the majority of Englishmen. All that contributed to the splendour of worship, all that had the faintest savour of ritualism, was condemned without mercy. The Puritan army saw in the organ an instrument of Satan. " A devil on those bagpipes," exclaimed Colonel Sands on hearing the organ in Rochester Cathedral; and as the prebendary endeavoured to drive back the invading forces, Sands discharged his pistol at him. At Chichester Cromwell's soldiers broke the organ-pipes with their battle-axes, and they behaved in the same way at Worcester, Norwich, Peterborough, Canterbury, and Winchester. The pipes of the organ of Westminster Abbey were bartered for pots of beer in the London taverns. In many a church and cathedral the sacerdotal ornaments and vestments were torn to pieces, the service-books destroyed, the statues of the saints demolished, and the stained-glass windows broken. Winchester Cathedral still bears the traces of the injuries inflicted upon it by these fanatics. The magnificent tomb of Bishop Wykeham, during whose episcopate the cathedral had been rebuilt, was, however, spared, thanks to a pure chance. The leader of the troops, Sir William Waller, was checked in his work of devastation by the memory of the time he had spent at Winchester School, of which Wykeham had been the founder. This fact would suffice to prove that the officers had their men well in hand, and that the orders for destruction were therefore given of set purpose. This same William Waller at Chichester, Sir Thomas Mauleverer at Ripon, the Earl of Essex at Worcester — merely to quote a few of the more notorious leaders — sanctioned their soldiers' acts of vandalism. It is only right to add that the soldiers were not always inspired by religious fanaticism alone; they were also prompted by a desire for loot. Evelyn alludes to their " hellish avarice " in his *Journal,* under the date August 19, 1654.

In 1647 the Long Parliament ordered the closing of all theatres, in terms most derogatory to the actors, who were declared to be " rogues " and ordered to be " apprehended and openly and publiquely whipt " if proved to have acted in stage-plays.

Oliver Cromwell, however, who was master for the moment, was not hostile to the cause of art. He loved music and received at his house the most skilful musicians of the day, whose talent he recompensed, though Heath, the author of the *Flagellum*, a scurrilous pamphlet attacking the memory of the Lord Protector, issued in 1665, alleges that the remuneration was wretched. This may be so, but it is certain that by his timely intervention Cromwell saved the organ of Magdalen College, Oxford, and had it secretly removed to the palace of Hampton Court. Carlyle relates that he wrote to the clergy of Ely Cathedral requesting them to refrain from singing the service, for fear the soldiers might take it upon themselves to reform the character of the religious celebrations according to their own ideas. Thanks to this request, Ely suffered but little. Lincoln Cathedral was within an ace of being handed over to the pickax of the housebreakers. Original Peart, who was mayor of Lincoln in 1650, and afterwards represented it in Parliament, pointed out to Cromwell that without its cathedral Lincoln would become one of the ugliest cities in England. There seems to be no doubt that the Lord Protector gave orders for the preservation of this magnificent building.

If sacred music suffered cruelly at the hands of the Puritan regime, secular music, though it certainly lost much of its vitality, did at any rate continue to exist; and had Cromwell's dictatorship lasted longer, it would probably have succeeded in winning for itself an almost normal, if not very active existence. Musicians gradually retrieved their position in the public estimation and managed to live on the proceeds of their profession. As early as 1652 John Playford, a bookseller and stationer of the Inner Temple, set up as a music-publisher. He was the true father of music-publishing, and rendered great services in this field.

In 1653 appeared the first book of *Ayres and Dialogues for One, Two and Three Voyces*, composed by Henry Lawes, whose name has already been mentioned in connexion with the masques. He was a pupil of Coperario, and had written the music for the songs in Milton's *Comus*, performed at Ludlow Castle in 1634. Childe, Webb, Coleman, and Simpson published various works, to which the public gave a favourable reception. Matthew Lock and Christopher Gibbons composed the music for Shirley's masque *Cupid and Death*, which numbered among its distinguished spectators the Portuguese ambassador. A little later, in 1656, Matthew Lock brought out his *Consort of three parts for viols*. The *Lessons* for the virginal of Bull, Gibbons, and other famous masters appeared about the same time.

The composition of church music had ceased. Spoken drama having been prohibited, the idea of musical drama was conceived. In May 1656 Henry Lawes, Coleman, George Hudson, and Henry Cooke, generally known as Captain Cooke, because he had risen to the rank of a captain in the royal army during the Civil War, joined forces in composing the music for Sir William Davenant's *First Day's Entertainment*, a strange composition in which declamation and music were mingled "in the fashion of the Ancients."

In this work Diogenes and Aristophanes, mounted on platforms adorned with gilding, could be heard arguing at length for and against theatrical performances. A Parisian and a Londoner were also to be heard holding forth upon the charms of their respective capitals. The speeches were preceded by music suited to the character of the speakers. Gloomy or gay, according as Diogenes or Aristophanes was to speak, and French or English in character, according as the subject was Paris or London, this curious work had Rutland House as its theatre; it was not intended for the great public, to which, indeed, it would have made little appeal. The object of the authors was to sound the feeling of the leading men in the Commonwealth. The experiment that they tried aroused no protest on the part of the Puritan authorities, and a little later Davenant was emboldened to produce *The Siege of Rhodes,* a work in which monologues were interspersed with dialogues in the recitative style. Each act was preceded by a symphony and ended in a chorus. *The Siege of Rhodes* was no more nor less than an opera, the formula for which was borrowed from Italy. Unfortunately we can form no idea of the musical value of these two works of Sir W. Davenant's, for the scores have never been discovered. Their literary value is but poor, so that the interest which they offer is purely historical, though its value is undeniable.

We have now come to the eve of the Restoration.

It should be stated that during Cromwell's Protectorship the monodic style struggled against the polyphonic style, not without success.

Is it not strange, and even paradoxical, that the Puritans should have condemned the part played by the organ and polyphonic religious music, the austerity of which would seem to have been in harmony with their doctrines, while they tolerated a lighter and even profane form of art?

During the dictatorship of Cromwell, one of whose high officials, the poet Milton, Latin secretary to the Council under the Commonwealth, was a great lover of music, a certain recrudescence in musical production did indeed make itself felt. But all the same, in passing from the year 1658, the date of the Protector's death, to 1660, that of Charles II's accession, we feel as though we were issuing from a region plunged in gloom and entering one flooded with light.

The fires of art, damped down by the Puritan regime, and only partially and timidly revived under Cromwell, blazed up again with even greater brilliance as soon as the reign of Charles II began. But the breath which rekindled them brought with it a whole host of moral miasmata. An odiously tyrannical rigorism was succeeded by an appalling licence; and a parade of vice took the place of an ostentatious show of real or assumed virtue. The court became a haunt of corruption.

The middle classes, of whom Samuel Pepys

is a well-known example, steered a middle course of reasonable respectability. The easy-going Pepys did not set up to be either a vicious man or a saint. He was not utterly averse from the pleasures of the bottle. One day he takes a solemn oath to abstain from strong drink — for a certain time. If he goes so far as to be unfaithful to his wife, he confesses his fault and confides his remorse to paper. He played the violin and flageolet, was a passionate lover of music, and wished to make those around him share his tastes. Finding his wife but a poor pupil, he recalled Thomas Tusser's words and taught his servant Mercer to sing. In his youth he was slightly tinged with the puritanism of the age, but he followed the development of religious ideas and showed signs of an increasingly lively sympathy with Catholicism. His religious zeal was accompanied, however, by a susceptibility to the fine clothes and pretty women that he saw at church, among whom were the favourites of Charles II. Lady Castlemaine's dresses filled him with delight. As an official occupying an important post — he was Secretary to the Admiralty — he acquired a very wide experience of men and things in the course of his relations with all classes of society, and judges them in his *Diary* with charming good humour and a wide indulgence both for others and for himself.

The finest characters were to be found among the Nonconformists: for example, a Milton, a Bunyan, or an Elwood.

The common people had not lost their sense of decency. A dense crowd besieged a London tavern at the window of which Sir Charles Sedley had appeared in the simplest attire, and in its fury was ready to seize him and give him a thrashing, so that Sir Charles was forced to beat a retreat.

But whatever the state of morals may have been at the period of the Restoration, social relations became more elastic and gained in confidence. The barriers between the aristocracy and the artistic world became less rigid. We find Captain Cooke playing at skittles with Lord Sandwich, and Lords Rochester, Falkland, Sunderland, and Lauderdale treating musicians with a familiarity that has nothing offensive about it. The Duke of Buckingham had a band of violinists in his pay; and the famous guitar-player Francesco Corbetti found an eager pupil in the Duke of York.

From the accession of Charles II onwards, fine singing was once more to be heard in the churches, accompanied by the notes of the organ. Pepys is careful to note these facts as early as July 8, 1660. The taste for music became more and more widespread among the middle classes. Pepys reports that at the time of the fire of London (1666), when the Thames was covered with boats during the salvage operations, one in every three of them contained a virginal. Musical instruments, of which customers had the free use, once more made their appearance in the barbers' shops, a custom alluded to in earlier days by Ben Jonson in *The Alchemist* and *The Silent Woman*. If we are to believe a couple of verses of a poem written in the eighteenth century and quoted by Naylor in *Shakespeare and Music*, it appears that the music performed on them was not always of a high quality, nor did the executants always display much skill:

> In former time 't hath been upbrayded thus
> That *Barbers'* musick was most *Barbarous*.

This pun was no doubt in keeping with the facts; but it is none the less true that music was a source of acute pleasure to the men of the sixteenth and seventeenth centuries, whether among nobles and great ladies or among the middle classes and commoners.

Musicks Hand-maide

Prefenting New and Pleafant LESSONS
FOR THE

Virginals or Harpfycon.

London, Printed for John Playford at his Shop in the Temple. 1663.

FRONTISPIECE FROM PLAYFORD'S
Musicks Hand-maide

On December 30, 1672, the *London Gazette* announced that John Banister, the violinist, had started some paying concerts. These concerts took place in his house, opposite the George Tavern, in the neighbourhood of Whitefriars, and began at four o'clock in the afternoon. They were evidently well attended, for they did not come to an end till the death of the founder, on October 3, 1679. Banister was buried in the cloisters of Westminster Abbey. It may be mentioned in passing that many of the tombstones there bear the names of musicians of the day, which is a sign that the musical profession was viewed with respect.

But it was King Charles II himself who gave the chief impulse to the movement. The frivolity, levity, cynicism, and vicious propensities of this prince have been judged with great severity by historians. With what cruel indifference he treated his wife, Catherine of Braganza! And yet during an illness which endangered the Queen's life he shed copious tears and used tender language to her in which his remorse was evident. Charles II's nature was extremely complex; he was indolent, yet brave when the occasion demanded it. Though in the pay of Louis XIV, he none the less showed on more than one occasion that he had a national sense. In a show-case in the British Museum may be seen a holograph letter, dated from the Palace of Whitehall, in which he orders captains of ships to insist that all nations shall salute the British flag. Selfish though he was, on many occasions he displayed feelings of humanity. And on certain points all historians are agreed: Charles II was witty and clever; he had the gift of talking well; he knew how to charm his company; above all, he possessed an artistic sense, and in particular a keen and lively appreciation of music.

On ascending the throne of his ancestors, Charles II thought fit to give music its part in the official ceremonies. Matthew Lock was given the task of composing the coronation march for sackbuts and cornets, which was to accompany his state procession from the Tower of London to the Palace of Whitehall on the eve of the coronation. Henry Lawes wrote and supervised the performance of the anthem *Zadok the Priest* for the coronation service. Besides Lawes and Lock, it was not long before the King summoned to his side those musicians who had escaped the troubles of the Revolution: Laniere, Coleman, Banister, Childe, Christopher Gibbons, and Captain Cooke. He showered favours upon them and found them remunerative posts. In so doing he was discharging a debt of gratitude to many who, at the risk of their lives, had given proof of a noble devotion to Charles I.

Special mention should be made in this connexion of Henry Lawes, Christopher Gibbons, and Cooke. Unfortunately the King's prodigality overtaxed the resources of the civil list, and he was often unable to keep the generous promises which he had rashly made.

Charles II showed great kindness to certain foreign musicians; for instance, Francesco Corbetti, whom he admitted as a member of his household and for whom he took pains to arrange a good marriage; John Baptist Draghi, an excellent harpsichord-player, who became organist to Catherine of Braganza on the death of Lock, in 1677; Baltzar of Lübeck, the famous violinist, who astounded his contemporaries, and notably Evelyn and Anthony Wood, by shifting up to the highest notes; Louis Grabu, an inferior musician, of whom Pepys records a somewhat unfavourable judgment, but who had the merit, in the eyes of Charles II, of being a Frenchman; Robert Cambert, organist at the church of Saint-Honoré, director of music to Anne of Austria, and composer of the *Pastorale*, played for the first time at the château of Issy in 1659, of *Ariane, Adonis, Pomone* (1671), and *Les Peines et les Plaisirs de l'Amour* (1671). Cambert, who had the honour to incur the jealousy of Lully, retired to England with bitterness in his heart, and died there in 1677, as master of the " King's Music." An article in the *Nouveau Mercure Galant* for April 1677 informs us that he received many favours from Charles II and the greatest noblemen about the court.

Very little of Cambert's work has survived. In consequence of a letter, dated May 18, 1880, from Mr. Charles T. Evans of the British Museum to J. B. Weckerlin, librarian of the Paris Conservatoire, it was for long believed that no manuscripts of Cambert's work had been preserved in the country where he ended his days. But in the course of a meeting of the Société Française de Musicologie held in Paris on June 20, 1927, Monsieur Tessier informed his colleagues that the British Museum catalogue of manuscript music, compiled by Barclay Squire, mentions a vocal air by this composer as existing in a manuscript belonging to the Department of Manuscripts. The catalogue of the Library of Westminster Abbey, compiled by the same eminent scholar, records the existence of another manuscript containing six other airs by Cambert — a small manuscript book, as we are informed by the courtesy of the Precentor, the Rev. Canon Nixon, entitled *Airs de différens compositeurs, 1678*. The titles of those by Cambert are: *En quel estat; Affreuse nuit; Sommeil doux; Hélas, vous demandez; Ah, qu'après les ennuys;* and *Des pleurs que je respand*. The first act of *Pomone* and the first act of *Les Peines et les Plaisirs de l'Amour,* edited by J. B. Weckerlin, prove that, though his merit is inferior to that of Lully, it is, none the less, far from negligible: in any case, he can claim the merit of having been the founder of French opera, and this fact entitles him to an important place in musical history.

Charles II sent for violinists from France and formed a band of twenty-four stringed instruments, exactly similar to the *Grande Bande* at the French court. The function of this band was to give court concerts and play during the royal banquets. The King gave Baltzar the position of conductor, in which he was succeeded on his death, in 1663, by John Banister. There were no court festivities at which music was not called upon to play a leading part. Almost every day was distinguished by an entertainment, and this fact, together with what was known of Charles II's somewhat licentious view of life, explains why he was nicknamed the Merry Monarch.

The Musicians' Company, dissolved at the Revolution, was reconstituted, and the theatres reopened. Shortly after his accession the King granted letters patent for the building of two new playhouses. One of these, situated in Catherine Street, Strand, on the very spot where Drury Lane Theatre is now to be found, bore the name of the King's Theatre, and had Thomas Killigrew as its manager. In 1671 it was burnt down, but was immediately replaced by another, the designs for which were entrusted to Sir Christopher Wren, the greatest architect of the day. The other, which was reserved for the Duke of York's players, had Sir William Davenant as its manager. In 1670–1 it was replaced by an elegant building adorned with a colonnade, under which coaches could drive, known as the Dorset Garden Theatre, because it was built on the site of the gardens of Dorset House. On the death of Sir William Davenant, his widow, his son Charles, and two of the principal actors, Harris and the famous Betterton, joined together to form a sort of managing committee. It was in one or the other of these theatres that most of the pieces for which Henry Purcell composed the incidental music were performed.

The conditions which we have just described were well calculated to create an atmosphere favourable to musical production; but the institution which did most to foster Purcell's genius and encourage it to develop and attain maturity was the Chapel Royal.

II

The Chapel Royal and Captain Cooke

THE CHAPEL ROYAL HAD BEEN REORGAN-
ized as early as the year 1660, when Captain Cooke was appointed Master. The date of
Cooke's death is surrounded with mystery. He is
known to have belonged to Charles I's Chapel
Royal, and we have already said that he enlisted
in the Royalist army. Under the Puritan regime
he settled in London and taught music. Evelyn
speaks with admiration of his talent as a singer,

noting in his Diary that "he is the best singer after the Italian manner of any in England." "Without doubt he hath the best manner of singing in the world," Pepys was to write later. Readers will remember that Henry Cooke was one of the collaborators in Sir William Davenant's *First Day's Entertainment*. He composed a good many anthems, of which Pepys was very fond, the music for the coronation service, and a hymn that was performed at St. George's Chapel, Windsor, on April 17, 1661 at the great chapter of the Order of the Garter. In 1670, on the death of Laniere, he was appointed Marshal of the Musicians' Company, and his own death took place on June 24, 1672.

Captain Cooke's merits as a composer are contested, and probably with reason. Dr. Charles Burney, in the third volume of his *History of Music* (p. 444), judges him with great severity, on the strength of a few secular compositions scattered through the collections of the period, and two or three songs published by Playford in the second part of his *Musical Companion*. He declares that Cooke was not qualified to discharge the distinguished functions entrusted to him by the confidence of his sovereign. But this assertion is in contradiction with the facts. We have no information about the methods adopted by Captain Cooke, but we know that by his activity and almost apostolic fervour he infused life into his surroundings. He made a careful choice among the boys who presented themselves as candidates for the Chapel Royal, and knew how to discern which of them were likely to do credit to his teaching. When one of his pupils whose voice had broken did not fulfil his expectations, he dissuaded him from following a musical career and used his influence, which was considerable, to find him employment suited to his ability. Under his wise and firm guidance the Chapel Royal became an artistic centre full of vitality, the influence of which was felt far beyond the limits of the capital. Many of his former pupils carried with them into the various counties the fruits of his solid musical education, and a high esteem for music. Setting aside Purcell, the best known of them are the following:

William Turner, born in 1651, a member of the choir of Lincoln Cathedral, afterwards a vicar choral of St. Paul's and a lay vicar of Westminster Abbey. He became a doctor of music in 1696 and died at the age of eighty-eight, after seventy years of married life.

Sampson Estwick, born in 1657, chaplain

of Christ Church, Oxford, appointed a minor canon of St. Paul's in 1692. In a sermon that he preached in the cathedral at Oxford, he treated of the uses of sacred music. He became vicar of St. Helen's, Bishopsgate, and afterwards rector of St. Michael's, Queenhithe, and died in 1739.

Henry Hall, poet and musician, born about 1655. He became organist first to Exeter and then to Hereford Cathedral, and died in 1707.

Michael Wise, born about 1648. Between 1668 and 1675 he was first organist and then choirmaster at Salisbury Cathedral. He next became a gentleman of the Chapel Royal and finally, in 1685, choirmaster at St. Paul's, after which he returned to Salisbury. He was of a quarrelsome disposition, as the following anecdote will show: On one occasion he left his house on a dark night after a quarrel with his wife, and came into collision with one of the watch. In the course of the dispute that ensued he received a blow on the head from a stick, of which he died in 1687. He was fond of improvising on the organ — so much so that he often resented the fact that the progress of divine service interfered with his improvisations.

Thomas Tudway, first bachelor and afterwards doctor of music, became organist at King's

College, Cambridge, in 1670, and afterwards at Pembroke College. One of his anthems was performed in King's College Chapel in the presence of Queen Anne, who granted him the honorary title of Composer and Organist to the Queen. He died in 1730, after collecting and transcribing a number of sacred compositions at the instance of Lord Harley, which fill six great quarto volumes and are included in the Harleian collection in the British Museum. He brought many unpleasantnesses upon himself owing to his caustic wit and mania for making puns of a satirical nature.

John Blow, born in Nottinghamshire about 1648, one of the most famous names in the history of English music. He gave proofs of extraordinary precocity. At the age of twenty-one he was appointed organist of Westminster Abbey, in which position he had had as his immediate predecessors Albertus Byrne and Christopher Gibbons.

Pelham Humphrey, born in 1647, who composed anthems while still a child. Charles II sent him to Paris to perfect his musical education. Humphrey stayed there for three years, receiving a grant of two hundred pounds the first year, a hundred pounds the second, and a hundred and

fifty pounds the third. He enjoyed the acquaint-
ance of Lully, whose works he studied. On his
return from France he took the oath as a gentleman of the Chapel Royal, succeeded to Captain
Cooke's post in 1672, was appointed Composer
in ordinary to the King's violins and conductor
of his band, and died in 1674 at the age of 27!

The object of these few biographical notes
is simply to introduce these composers to the
reader. We propose to return to them in the
critical section of this work.

The first three of them, William Turner,
Sampson Estwick, and Henry Hall, who belonged to the ecclesiastical world, were highly
cultivated men, which justifies us in supposing
that the pupils in Cooke's school did not confine
themselves to the study of music. The late Rev.
H. F. Westlake was strongly of opinion that
Latin was included in their curriculum.

III

Henry Purcell

A WRITER IN THE *RADIO TIMES* FOR SEPTEM-
ber 1925, Dr. Purcell-Taylor, states that
Henry Purcell's ancestors were of French origin,
though the authority for this statement is not
given, and inquiries made by the present writer
have failed to elicit it. If any weight is to be
given to Dr. Purcell-Taylor's statement, they
took refuge in England after the massacre of St.
Bartholomew. They were glass-blowers by pro-

fession, but, having suffered from the monopoly established by the English Government, they turned to music, for they were gifted musicians.

According to Dr. Grattan, Purcell's ancestors were Irish. But there are wills going back as far as 1547 preserved at Somerset House that refer to some Pursells or Purshells as the heirs of David Fyssher of Salopp Sherman and of John Fyssher, a gentleman of the Chapel Royal under Henry VII, Henry VIII, and Edward VI, which would seem to justify the theory that the composer's ancestors were natives of Shropshire. There is a portrait of Purcell by Clostermann under the engraving of which appears the following coat of arms: Barry wavy of six argent and gules; on a bend sable three boars' heads couped of the first. Does the fact that the composer used these arms justify us in stating that he was connected with the Purcells of Onslow, Shropshire? Dr. Cummings is disposed, on the strength of these wills, to connect Purcell with David and John Fyssher. Hart has no hesitation in regarding the Shropshire Purcells as the real ancestors of the English master, but adduces no proofs in support of his theory. After repeated efforts to achieve a satisfactory solution of the problem, we can only concur in the judgment of Mr. Dennis Arundell, Purcell's most recent biographer, as stated in his excellent book: " Despite various attempts to solve the mystery of his ancestry, none of the fantastic tales or hopeful theories has produced any definite facts, and the earliest detail that can be proved to belong to Henry Purcell's family is that Edward, his brother, was born in 1653." The question of Purcell's pedigree can be studied by those interested in the subject in *Collectanea Top. et Gen.*, VII, 244, and VIII, 17, 20, and in *Harl. Mss.* 6153 at the British Museum.

Henry Purcell's father, whose Christian name was also Henry, was one of the gentlemen of the Chapel Royal. He became a member of the choir of Westminster Abbey, Master of the Children in connexion with it, and afterwards music-copyist to the Abbey. It was the task of the music-copyists to reconstitute the libraries of sacred music that had suffered from the ravages of the Puritan regime. Lastly, Henry Purcell senior was a member of the Royal Band. He had a fine voice, was a skilful performer on the lute, and in case of need could have acted as organist to the Abbey. In short, he was one of those musicians who are not distinguished for any brilliant endowments, but whose wide experience, added to their natural gifts, renders constant and invaluable service. A song for three voices, entitled " Sweet Tyranness, I now resign my heart," and published in 1667 by Playford in his *Musical Companion*, is attributed to him; but it is also attributed to his son Henry. Purcell senior did not long enjoy the material and moral advantages of an appointment in the Royal Band. He was nominated in 1663 and died in 1664, leaving three sons, Edward, Henry, and Daniel, and a daughter Katherine.

Edward, who was born in 1653, received an appointment in the Royal Household as gentleman-usher, and afterwards served with distinction as an officer in the English army in Ireland and Flanders, rising to the rank of lieutenant-colonel and taking part in the siege of Gibraltar. His health having failed, not so much owing to age as to the hardships of the life that he had led, he retired to a position in the household of the Earl of Abingdon, and died in 1717. He was buried in the choir of the church of Wytham, near Oxford; and his tombstone bears an inscription in which the various stages of his career are enumerated in moving, though sober, terms.

Daniel was probably born in 1660. After consulting his elder brother he embraced the profession of music. He was organist to Magdalen College, Oxford, and his compositions include some anthems, an ode to St. Cecilia, incidental music to dramatic works by Colley Cibber, Settle, Tom d'Urfey, Motteux, and Farquhar, a second ode to St. Cecilia (1707), and sonatas for flute and bass viol. He died in 1717, having occupied the position of organist at St. Andrew's, Holborn, for four years. In spite of the large number of works bearing his name, he has left very little mark upon the history of music. Hawkins goes so far as to say that he had more skill as a punster than as a composer. But Daniel Purcell had at least the merit of loving and admiring his brother Henry.

Many points in the life of Henry Purcell are still obscure; and, in the first place, the exact date of his birth. His name does not appear in the baptismal register of the parish of St. Margaret's, Westminster, where he certainly first saw the light, nor does the Rate-book of that parish contain his father's name. One of his biographers, Dr. William H. Cummings, states that he was undoubtedly born in 1658. This date, which seems to be confirmed by two documents to which we shall refer below, is the one generally adopted, and there is good reason to believe that it is the right one.

Dr. Cummings locates the house in which our musician was born in St. Ann's Lane, leading into Old Pye Street. He bases his statement upon a sketch made by R. W. Withal on April 15, 1845, to which certain descriptive details are appended. Trusting in this assertion, let us visit the spot, full of pleasant anticipation.

St. Ann's Lane does indeed still exist. It is a deserted alley, rendered more deserted still by comparison with the neighbouring main streets, which swarm with little ragamuffins. The alley, which is paved with flagstones, is some hundred yards long, about five yards wide at the Old Pye Street end, and three yards at the other end, with a gutter running down the middle of it. It is shut off by five stone posts at one end and three at the other, so that it is inaccessible to wheeled traffic, and is flanked on the south by high brick buildings blackened with soot — bath-houses, shops, etc. Looking towards Old Pye Street, we may see on the right a modest house that seems to show no signs of life. It is not even in a line with the other houses, but seems to be shrinking from notice behind a wall,

from which it is separated by a tiny courtyard.
Can this be Purcell's house? We gaze at it in a
contemplative mood. But a doubt enters our
mind. Its shape does not correspond with the
description given by Dr. Cummings. Uneasy as
to the result of his explorations, and yet with a
secret hope that it was Cummings who was at
fault, the present writer wended his way home-
wards and wrote a letter to the Rev. H. F. Westlake, for whom Westminster had no secrets. The
reverend gentleman was so kind as to reply that
there are no houses still standing in Westminster
old enough to have witnessed Purcell's birth,
except within the precincts of the Abbey — but
it was not there that the composer first saw the
light. A house once occupied by him in Bowling
Alley — now Tufton Street — was pulled down
a few years ago. Mr. Sydney Nicholson, until recently organist to Westminster Abbey, has in
his possession a bookcase made of wood from
this house.

Henry Purcell may have passed his earliest
days in St. Ann's Lane, but we must resign ourselves to the fact that the house in which he was
born is no longer to be seen there. Even if he was
not born in this street, it is certain (and this is
the opinion of another of his biographers, John

F. Runciman, who is, however, always very guarded in accepting any definite statements about Purcell's life) that the city of Westminster may boast of having heard his first wails. Our ideas are still further confused by the *London Gazette* of June 7, 1683, which gives the place of the composer's residence at that time as being in St. Ann's Lane, " beyond Westminster Abbey." Is this the house alluded to in Cummings's book, the existence of which has not been spared by the municipal authorities?

Henry Purcell received his first notions about music from his father. On the death of the latter the child was taken under the protection of his uncle Thomas, an excellent man, who treated him with a truly paternal affection. In a letter addressed by Thomas Purcell in 1679 to the Rev. John Gostling, a minor canon of Canterbury, he alludes to his nephew as his " son." And here we may insert in parenthesis a few remarks on the Rev. John Gostling, whose name will recur more than once in the course of this work. He had a magnificent bass voice of exceptional depth, and it was for him that Henry Purcell wrote his famous anthem " They that go down to the sea in ships " (Psalm cvii. 23). Charles II highly appreciated the talent, voice, and good humour of the Rev. J. Gostling. Dr. Cummings relates that one day the King presented him with a silver egg full of guineas, "having heard that eggs were good for the voice." "You may say what you like about your nightingales," exclaimed the sovereign on another occasion. "I have a *Gosling* who surpasses them all." The pun is a poor one, but has the advantage of showing us the tone of amiable familiarity with which Charles II would speak of a musician.

Like his brother, Thomas Purcell was a most expert musician, and, like him, a gentleman of the Chapel Royal. On the death of Henry Lawes he became lute-player to the court. In 1672 he shared with Pelham Humphrey the honour of conducting the King's band of twenty-four violins, for which he was to be paid two hundred pounds a year. Our authority for this statement is a schedule of salaries drawn up by his own hand, and preserved in the archives of the Royal Society of Musicians. Pepys informs us in his *Diary*, for December 19, 1666, that the musicians were paid so irregularly that they were "ready to starve." The accounts of the Treasurer of the Great Wardrobe show us that Thomas Purcell received no salary for four years and nine months. As conductor of the twenty-four violins, Thomas Purcell enjoyed more extensive powers than his colleague, on account of his age. Henry's guardian was appointed Marshal of the Musicians' Company in 1672, when Captain Cooke was forced to resign on grounds of health. Certain of his compositions are still included in the repertory of English choir-schools.

By his uncle's influence, young Henry Purcell was admitted as one of the Children of the Chapel Royal. Dr. Cummings is inclined to think that the vocal trio " Sweet Tyranness, I now resign my heart," which we mentioned in connexion with H. Purcell senior, is by H. Purcell junior. The simplicity with which the music is written points to a child's style rather than that of an adult. However that may be, young Henry showed signs of striking precocity as a composer. In 1670, at the age of twelve, he wrote an ode on the occasion of the King's birthday, which has as its title: *The address of the Children of the Chapel Royal to the King, and their master, Captain Cooke, on his Majesties Birthday, A.D. 1670, Composed by Master Purcell, one of the children of the said Chapel.*

Was it Henry Purcell who, at the age of fourteen, composed the incidental music for

Shakspere's tragedy of *Macbeth,* arranged in his own fashion by Sir William Davenant and adapted to the taste of the period? Sir William intended this work for performance at the Dorset Garden Theatre, but was prevented by death from carrying out his purpose. It was his widow who did so four years later, meeting with such success as to cover her outlay twice over, as we are informed by Downes, a contemporary writer, in his *Roscius Anglicanus, or an Historical Review of the Stage.* Or should this music be attributed to Matthew Lock?

Relying on the fact that there is a copy of this work in existence in Purcell's hand (it formed part of his own library), Dr. Cummings is strongly inclined to accept the former hypothesis. But the argument he advances does not strike us as conclusive. We know that H. Purcell transcribed a number of works, and notably an anthem composed by Pelham Humphrey; and we have several works of Purcell's copied by John Blow. Dr. Cummings adds that there are copies of the *Macbeth* music in existence bearing the name of the young musician. Neither this second argument, nor the testimony in support of this theory of Samuel Arnold, William Hayes, and Philip Hayes, doctors of music in the eighteenth

century, seems to us convincing; indeed, there
are abundant examples of such errors con-
secrated by tradition. On the other hand, Downes
credits Matthew Lock with the music which
serves to interpret Sir William Davenant's piece.
We merely confine ourselves to stating the problem. All that we feel justified in saying is that
there are certain pages in the work in question
which seem, by the simplicity of the writing, to
point to the hand of a novice; and these pages
have also a certain savour, a certain grace, which
recall the style of Purcell. We may instance in
particular " We should rejoice when good Kings
bleed," with its decided rhythm, and " Let's
dance upon the heath," which is worthy of note
for its pleasing pastoral character.

It is also important to record that before
July 14, 1672, the date of Captain Cooke's death,
Henry Purcell had composed several sacred
pieces, and in particular some anthems. In a revised form — revised, however, by the hand of
the composer — these are still sung in the
churches of England, and will long continue
to be.

Captain Cooke had encouraged the child's
earliest efforts and intelligently directed his first
steps. It does not seem that the child had much

left to learn from him at the stage which he had now reached.

Pelham Humphrey, Captain Cooke's successor, was certainly the man best able to satisfy the aspirations of a growing lad towards novelty in musical expression. In his master Purcell was able to appreciate fine sensibilities akin to his own. He soon realized what rich resources he would find in this receptive nature, matured by long intercourse with Lully and by a thorough study of the Italians of whom Lully was the musical heir or rival. When Pelham Humphrey died, two years almost to a day after Captain Cooke, his place was taken by John Blow. Pelham Humphrey had opened up wide vistas before Purcell's eyes; his chief service was to reveal to him the resources of the monodic style. John Blow, while perfecting the young man's technique on the organ, gave him a thorough training in all the difficulties of the polyphonic style.

The composer's voice had now broken, and his work as one of the Children of the Chapel Royal was therefore at an end; but he did not sever his connexion with the Chapel, and continued to pass his life under the protecting wing of Westminster Abbey.

In 1676 he was appointed to the position of

copyist to the Abbey, from which he retired in
1678 in order to find time for his own work. In
1677 he was appointed Composer in ordinary to
His Majesty's violins, with a salary, in the place
of Matthew Lock, deceased. In 1680 he became
regular organist at Westminster Abbey, his talent
thus receiving public and official recognition.
There is a touching tradition to the effect that
John Blow made way before the overwhelming
superiority of his pupil. But there is no proof of
this magnanimous action extant. Possibly Blow
was discreetly pressed to yield his place to Purcell, and complied smilingly with a good grace.
But this is a point which may perhaps never be
cleared up. It is not improbable that Blow wished
to pay a tribute to this pupil who was the pride
of his career. He insisted that the words " Henry
Purcell's master " should be carved upon his
tombstone as a title to fame. He had, moreover,
a delicate artistic conscience and a great natural
kindliness. It is hard to believe that, for all his
kindliness and artistic conscientiousness, Blow
would not have felt and displayed some resent-
ment against Purcell, had the latter been guilty
of a serious breach of delicacy in his relations
towards him. As a matter of fact, the relations
between the two men never ceased to be friendly,

and even affectionate. In 1694 — that is to say, fourteen years after his appointment as organist to the Abbey — Purcell, in revising the twelfth edition of John Playford's *Introduction to the Skill of Music,* hailed John Blow as " one of the greatest masters in the world."

In all probability Henry Purcell married in 1680. In 1682 he was appointed organist to the Chapel Royal, a well-paid post, which was a cause for rejoicing to the young couple.

Among the duties which devolved upon the composer there was one which would not seem to have been very absorbing and is certainly somewhat curious. According to a document dated June 10, 1673, and found among the archives of the King's music, Henry Purcell was appointed " as keeper, maker, mender, repayrer and tuner of the regalls, organs, virginalls, flutes and recorders, and all other kind of wind instruments whatsoever, in ordinary and without fee, to His Majesty, and assistant to John Hingston, and, upon the death or other avoydance of the latter, to come in ordinary with salary." Hingston died in 1683, and Henry Purcell automatically became " Organ-Maker and Keeper." This document was discovered by the Rev. H. Cart de Lafontaine and published in his interest-

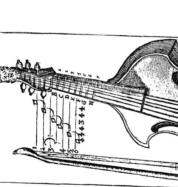

A BRIEF
INTRODUCTION
To the Playing on the
Treble-Violin.

THE *Treble-Violin* is a chearful and spritely Instrument, and much practised of late, some by Book, and some without; which of these two is the best way, may easily be resolved: To learn to Play by *Rote* or *Ear*, without Book, is the way never to Play more than what may be gain'd by hearing another Play, which may soon be forgot; but on the contrary, he which

F 4   Learns

A VIOL DA GAMBA AND A TREBLE VIOLIN,
FROM PLAYFORD'S *Introduction*

ing work *The King's Musick*. We agree with
John F. Runciman in considering it to be genuine.

Besides the address to King Charles II and
the anthems already mentioned, we must add to
the list of Purcell's compositions before the year
1680 an ode in memory of Matthew Lock (1677)
and various pieces published by Playford in his
collection of *Choyce Airs* in 1676 and 1679.

Before going on to speak of Purcell's dramatic works we feel it necessary to define their
general characteristics. We must once and for
all reject as improper the term " operas," which
has often been applied to them. They are plays,
in which the action is accompanied by incidental
music. This incidental music sometimes provides
scope for an overture, interlude, ballet airs, minuets, rondos, sarabands, jigs, chaconnes, hornpipes, and dances in three-time (³⁄₂) played at a
moderate pace; at times it also allows scope for
recitatives, vocal airs, duets, trios, and choruses.
We shall see later what was the extent of Purcell's
collaboration in the dramatic works that bear
his name. Littré defines opera as follows: a dramatic poem set to music, and more especially a
lyrical poem on a grand scale composed of recitatives, songs, and dances, without speeches or
spoken dialogues. As a matter of fact Purcell

wrote only one work answering to this definition: *Dido and Æneas.*

Mistakes due to relying upon the composer's earliest biographers have been made with regard to the date at which certain of his dramatic works were composed; and these errors have died hard. It was believed that the date at which the piece was printed or performed for the first time was the same as that at which the incidental music was written. If this had been so, then in 1676 Purcell would have composed the music for *Epsom Wells, The Libertine* (the prototype of Mozart's *Don Juan*), two comedies of Shadwell's, and Dryden's tragedy of *Aurengzebe.* The learned musical writer Mr. Barclay Squire, in his work on *Purcell's Dramatic Music,* puts forward other dates, and supports his conclusions by solid arguments. According to Mr. Barclay Squire, the music for *Epsom Wells* was composed in 1693, that of *The Libertine* in 1692 or 1695. With regard to *Aurengzebe* he writes: " The first performance took place, according to Genest, in the year 1675; but the first edition is dated 1676. As a matter of fact no music by Purcell for *Aurengzebe* is in existence, except perhaps one song, and this song was certainly interpolated at a date subsequent to 1676."

Abdelazer, or the Moor's Revenge, a tragedy by Mrs. Aphra Behn, was performed for the first time in 1677 at the Dorset Garden Theatre. But it should not be inferred that the music written for it by Purcell belongs to the same year. Cibber informs us in his *Apology* that the piece was revised on April 4, 1695, and it is to this year that we should assign the composer's share in the work. The mature quality of this work of Purcell's points to the fact that it is not a youthful production.

Dido and Æneas was not the first opera composed in England. The reader will recall what we said about *The Siege of Rhodes.* But the musical interest of the work, its nobility of style, and the grandeur and pathos with which it is inspired entitle *Dido and Æneas* to be regarded as the first opera worthy of the name produced in the country. The libretto is by Nahum Tate.

Floods of ink have been poured out with regard to the date at which this opera appeared. It was printed in 1841 on behalf of the Musical Antiquarian Society and edited by Sir George Macfarren, who fixes the date of the first performance as 1675, appealing to the authority of Professor Edward Taylor. Dr. Rimbault was in favour of the same date, though Hawkins had adopted that of 1677.

At the head of the libretto could be read the following title: *An opera performed at Mr. Josias Priest's Boarding-school at Chelsey, by young gentlewomen, the words made by Mr. Nat. Tate. The musick composed by Mr. Henry Purcell.*

Now, there is an advertisement in the *London Gazette* for November 22–5, 1680 which runs as follows: " Josias Priest, dancing-master, who kept a boarding-school of gentlewomen in Leicester Fields, is removed to the Great schoolhouse at Chelsey, that was Mr. Portman's."

This announcement, to which Hawkins alludes in a foot-note, attracted the attention of musical historians. Dr. Rimbault set the example of a conversion, now shown to be necessary, by declaring that Purcell's *Dido and Æneas* could not have been performed before 1680.

" There are good reasons," he adds, " for believing that this work was performed in that year, 1680, probably at the end of the Christmas holidays." As we see, Dr. Rimbault did not feel bound to assert this fact outright. The date 1680 was the one accepted until, as a result of his untiring investigations, Mr. Barclay Squire pro-

nounced in favour of the year 1689, or of some
year very near 1689, and backed up his conclusion
by arguments of undeniable weight, as may be
seen by referring to the essay on Purcell cited
above.

In 1678 an adaptation by Thomas Shadwell
of Shakspere's *Timon of Athens* was produced
under the title of *The History of Timon of
Athens, the man-hater*. A masque was interpolated in it, for which Purcell supplied an overture of a very elaborately developed character,
solos, duets, trios, and choruses. In this masque
we see Bacchus and Cupid disputing for su-
premacy, and finally arriving at a reconciliation
by resolving to unite their beneficent influence.
The work winds up with *A Curtain tune on a
Ground* — that is, an air played as the curtain
falls, on a reiterated bass figure — in other words,
a chaconne.

And here we may state, in parenthesis, that
a chaconne is a melody, most usually in three-
time, composed upon a bass figure four bars
long, which recurs as many times as the verses
or variations of which the chaconne is made up.
It hardly differs from the passacaglia. The passacaglia is slightly slower, and begins on the third
beat of the bar, whereas the chaconne begins

on the first. In the passacaglia the bass frequently blends with the higher parts in a contrapuntal tissue. And, lastly, it is generally in a minor key.

Does Purcell's music for the *Masque of Timon* date from the year 1678, as has been alleged? Once more Mr. Barclay Squire steps in: in his opinion, it does not.

Almost all musical historians are agreed with regard to the date, or at least, in certain cases, the approximate date of those dramatic works in which H. Purcell collaborated after 1679.

In 1680 appeared *Theodosius, or the Force of Love,* a tragedy by Nathaniel Lee, and *The Virtuous Wife,* a comedy by Tom d'Urfey, in which the assistance of our composer was called in. According to the conclusions of the preceding pages, it was in *Theodosius* that Purcell made his debut in writing for the theatre. His great career as a composer really begins in 1680, from which date onwards he produced an uninterrupted series of works, which ceased only with his life.

It was now that he inaugurated the series of odes dedicated to King Charles II, or else to his brother the Duke of York, who afterwards succeeded him on the throne as James II. These odes are known as Welcome Songs. Their musical scheme consists of an opening piece for strings, most often entitled a symphony, besides solos, duets, and trios, and choruses accompanied by the strings and sometimes by the organ.

It was the first of these Welcome Songs, *Welcome, Vicegerent of the Mighty King,* which greeted King Charles on his return to Windsor on September 9, 1680.

The second was probably composed in homage to the King on his return to London on October 12, 1681, after his stay at Newmarket. Luttrell, who kept a diary, like Evelyn and Pepys, notes that on this occasion the bells were rung at night and there were bonfires in many places. In this Welcome Song occurs the graceful melody " Swifter, Isis, swifter flow," followed by a chorus in which the same melody is repeated in four-part harmony. Charles II was very fond of this ode, which may have contributed towards the composer's promotion to the much-coveted position of organist to the Chapel Royal.

In May 1682 the Duke of York returned to London at the expiry of his service as Lord High Commissioner in Scotland. He too was welcomed back to the capital by bonfires and bell-ringing, as well as by H. Purcell's third Welcome Song, to the words " What shall be done on behalf of the man? "

The poem contains transparent allusions to the ruin of the hopes of Monmouth, a natural son of Charles II, who, with the aid of the restless, intriguing Shaftesbury, aspired towards excluding the Duke of York from the throne in hopes of his own advancement. The significance of the following two verses of the ode is unmistakable:

And now every tongue shall make open confession
That York, royal York, is the next in succession.

In 1682 Henry Purcell again composed an ode for the festivities in honour of the new Lord Mayor of London, Sir William Pritchard. The ode was performed on September 30.

October 22 was marked by a fourth Welcome Song, dedicated to the King and the Duke of York. This time Charles II's entry into London does not seem to have aroused the same enthusiasm as before; at any rate, Luttrell makes no particular comment upon the event. The song opens with the words: " The summer's absence unconcerned we bear " — an allusion to the King's annual absence from town and his summer residence at Newmarket.

In 1683, as if the composition of these odes — not to speak of a host of sacred works — were not enough to occupy him, Henry Purcell published by subscription a first series of pieces of chamber music, upon which his fame partly rests. The *London Gazette* for May 24 announces that on June 11 a collection of twelve sonatas " for three Parts — two Violins and Base — to the Harpsecord or Organ," will be supplied to subscribers, at a price of ten shillings; after June 11 the collection was to cost fifteen shillings. It is in a second notice about the publication, in the *London Gazette* for June 7, that the mention of St. Ann's Lane as the composer's place of residence occurs. The collection was printed and sold by J. Playford and J. Carr " at the Temple, Fleet Street," but does not seem to have brought its author much profit.

Purcell himself composed a preface for this collection, to which it is important to draw special attention; for it throws light upon the master's sentiments with regard to Italian and French music. He states that he has " faithfully endeavoured a just imitation of the most fam'd Italian masters; principally to bring the Seriousness and gravity of that sort of Musick [i.e., chamber music] into vogue and reputation among our countrymen, whose humour 'tis time now should begin to loath the levity and balladry of our neighbours [the French]." Towards the end of the preface there is a passage in which Purcell alludes to his use of technical terms unfamiliar to English executants, such as *Adagio* and *Grave*, *Presto*, *Largo*, *Vivace*, and *Piano*.

Among the evidence that has served to determine the date of Purcell's birth, we may mention the portrait that adorns the first-violin part of the sonatas. Beneath the portrait is the inscription: " *Vera effigies Henrici Purcell, Ætat. Suæ*, 24 [The true likeness of Henry Purcell at the age of twenty-four]."

This collection of twelve sonatas is dedicated to King Charles II. It was hardly in circulation when Purcell brought out a nuptial ode, *From hardy climes*, on the occasion of the marriage of Prince George of Denmark and the Princess Anne, daughter of the Duke of York, who became Queen of England on the death of William III.

In June of this same year, 1683, the unsuccessful plot came to light that is known to history as the Rye House Plot, because the conspirators used to meet at a miller's house. This event finds a melodious echo in the fifth Welcome Song:

Fly, bold Rebellion, make haste and be gone!
Victorious in Counsel, great Charles has returned.
The plot is displayed, and the traitors, some flown,
And some to Avernus by Justice thrown down.

The fifth Welcome Song concludes with a most effective seven-part chorus, to the words: "Welcome to all those wishes fulfilled." The date of its performance was either September 25, the date on which the King returned from Winchester, or October 20, on his return from Newmarket.

In November appeared three odes close upon one another in praise of St. Cecilia, the patron saint of music, " whose memory is honoured annually by a public festival organized on that day (November 22) by masters and friends of music both in England and foreign countries." This festival was of a purely secular character, in which it differed from those initiated by the " *Puy de Musique* " at Evreux at the end of the sixteenth century. Even before 1683, celebrations had taken place in England on November 22 in honour of St. Cecilia. " Music meetings " had been held at the Stationers' Hall, London, at which Captain Cooke had sung and played on the theorbo, and Pelham Humphrey had had a song performed, followed by a chorus, to the words: " How well doth this Harmonious Meeting prove! " According to Pepys, it was on November 22 that violins were introduced at the Chapel Royal for the first time. But it was not till 1683 that the Feast of St. Cecilia was regularly instituted. H. Purcell had the honour of officially inaugurating a celebration, in which he was followed by John Blow, William Turner, and Draghi. From the Revolution of 1688 till 1703 the festival assumed a religious character, being opened by an anthem and a sermon, which had to be a defence of sacred music. It was on such an occasion that in 1696 Sampson Estwick preached the sermon to which we have already alluded, taking as his text St. Paul's words: " Teaching and admonishing one another in psalms and hymns and spiritual songs, singing with grace in your hearts to the Lord " (Colossians iii. 16).

The first ode to St. Cecilia, *Welcome to all the Pleasures*, was composed by H. Purcell to words by Christopher Fishburn; the second, *Raise, raise the Voyce*, to an anonymous poem; and the third to some Latin words.

The sixth ode or Welcome Song has as its

title: *On the King's return to Whitehall after his Summer's progress.* This work was performed in September 1684. In it Charles II is represented as a messenger of peace with an olive-branch, and is compared to the dove sent forth from the ark.

In this year (1684) there took place a sort of artistic and commercial duel in which Purcell became implicated. The point at issue was the building of an organ for the Temple Church. There was a competition between two famous organ-builders of the period, Renatus Harris and Smith, generally known as " Father Smith," to distinguish him from his nephews, who worked with him; and two organs were set up. Harris selected John Baptist Draghi as his representative to show off his organ, while Smith had recourse to the good offices of Purcell, so that Harris was defeated. John Blow also took part in the contest on the side of Smith.

In 1685 Charles II died, and the composer had henceforth to offer his homage to his successor, James II. The coronation festivities were approaching. It was now that Purcell found an opportunity to justify his title of Organ-maker, at least in appearance, by supervising the construction in Westminster Abbey of a small supplementary organ intended to support the choirs. For this he received the sum of thirty-four pounds, twelve shillings, paid out of the secret-service money.

Two anthems by Purcell were performed at the coronation service: *I was glad when they said unto me* (Psalm cxxii. 1); and *My heart is inditing a good matter* (Psalm xlv. 1). Purcell joined the choir for the occasion, and took a bass part, together with John Blow, Childe, and Staggins. This Staggins, who now appears for the first time, was a violinist in King Charles's "Band." His name occurs in the list of salaries that we mentioned in connexion with Thomas Purcell.

On October 14, 1685 the King's birthday was celebrated, according to Luttrell, to the accompaniment of bonfires and bell-ringing.

This event was commemorated by a fresh ode of Purcell's: *Why, why are all the Muses mute?* and it contains allusions to the fate of Monmouth. James II, who appears under the form of Cæsar, annihilates the monster of revolt and hurls it down into the hell from which it had emerged. It is of importance to note that in this ode Purcell did not adopt the traditional plan. The symphony, with which the composition had

hitherto opened, comes after a solo for the alto
voice and the chorus which follows it. But in the
ode or Welcome Song for 1686 — *Ye tuneful
Muses, raise your heads* — as in his ninth and last
work of this sort, the composer once more con-
forms to established usage by restoring the symphony to its place at the beginning of the piece.

Between the eighth and ninth of these odes
Purcell wrote a pastoral elegy on the death of
John Playford's son at the age of twenty-one,
the words of which were by Nahum Tate.

The ninth ode (1687), *Sound the trumpet,
beat the drum,* is particularly brilliant. According to some manuscripts a part is introduced for
the drum and trumpet, in keeping with the
words. The ode contains six- and seven-part
choruses of magnificent sonority. In it are also
to be found the delightful duet " Let Cæsar and
Urania live! " and the grand chaconne in F major, which in the episode in F minor passes into
a mood of boundless melancholy, only to end in
a splendid, heroic rhythm calculated to leave the
listener under the impression of a final blaze of
glory. This ode, *Sound the trumpet, beat the
drum,* is one of those works of art that cast a
last resplendent ray upon a dynasty soon to expire. What a contrast the poet's panegyric and

the magnificence of the music, on the one hand, and the fate which awaited the prince, on the other! For in 1688 James II was driven from his throne and forced to seek refuge on foreign soil. Luttrell reports that in 1687 instructions were given that no bonfires were to be lit in the streets on the occasion of the King's birthday. Possibly James II felt how unpopular he was becoming, and dreaded hostile demonstrations.

The words of these royal odes are anonymous, with the exception of the sixth, *From those serene and rapturous joys,* in which they are the work of Thomas Flatman, and are certainly not devoid of real elegance. These odes are written in the irregular " Pindaric " style, and bear witness to the taste of the age for strained inversions, personified abstractions, and a blend of mythological reminiscences with Christian allusions, while the thought is expressed in hyperbolical terms. They are not, however, devoid of a certain historic interest. The nine Welcome Songs form a musical achievement imposing not only in volume, but in their artistic value. They fill three hundred and sixty-eight pages of the great edition published by the Purcell Society, and not one of them is less than forty pages in length.

But would it not be more correct to say that the terms in which the poets who composed the words of the Welcome Songs expressed their ideas *appear* hyperbolical nowadays? As a matter of fact, Charles II never ceased to be popular. He had been received with transports of joy and frantic applause in 1660 when he made his progress through London from the Tower to the Palace of Whitehall. The Restoration, to quote Lavisse's *Histoire de France,* was like " a resumption of the traditional life of the nation, which had been interrupted by a nightmare." The adventurous life that Charles II had led before coming to the throne, his misfortunes, and his acts of bravery increased to an extraordinary extent the prestige conferred upon him by his right to the crown, and caused him to appear surrounded by a halo of romance, which exercised an irresistible attraction over the masses. In spite of his faults and mistakes, he was always loved by the people, who remained indifferent to political complications. The discovery of the Rye House Plot was greeted with demonstrations of royalist enthusiasm, and when Russell, one of the chief conspirators, was executed, there were people who dipped their handkerchiefs in his blood as a sign of joy.

As for James II, he too enjoyed popular favour at first. It was not till after repeated acts of violence and breaches of legality on his part that the balance was upset between two feelings which are equally strong in the English: their loyalty, and their attachment to constitutional guarantees.

Henry Purcell lived in an age torn by religious passion. Most political questions were very closely bound up with points of theological doctrine. The measures adopted by James II, of which the implacable Jeffreys was the instrument — measures inspired by his Roman Catholic convictions — contributed in no small degree towards his fall. Charles II had been strongly attracted towards Roman Catholicism, but had succeeded in concealing his tendencies. It was only in secret that he received extreme unction upon his death-bed, at the hands of John Huddlestone, a Benedictine monk. His policy of compromise was a constant source of embarrassment to certain members of the Church of England. The ranks of the clergy contained more than one Vicar of Bray — the hero of the famous song, whose conception of religious life and the forms of worship was inspired by considerations of a prudent opportunism.

Entirely absorbed in his artistic task, Purcell did not formally attach himself to any political party; but at the period of his biography that we have now reached (1687–8), he unwittingly played a part in politics that was not without its importance. He had composed a "Quickstep," which appeared in 1686 in *The Delightful Companion, or Choice New Lessons for the Recorder or Flute.* In that same year James II appointed as Lord-Lieutenant of Ireland General Talbot, who had made himself hated by the Protestants on account of his oppressive measures. A doggerel poem was written to express this hatred for his administration, which became known by the name of *Lilliburlero,* because the refrain contained the words: *Lero, lero, lilli burlero.* Nor did it spare the King, as may be judged from the following couplets:

> Dere was an old prophecy found in a bog:
> "Ireland shall be ruled by an ass and a dog."

> And now dis prophecy is come to pass
> For Talbot's de dog, and King James is de ass.

These verses went the round among the masses; but their success would perhaps have been shortlived, and they would have fallen into oblivion, had not music lent them wings.

The words of *Lilliburlero* were set to the music of the " Quickstep," and its swinging rhythm made them popular. Thanks to Purcell's music, *Lilliburlero* became the rallying-cry of the Protestants, and was one of the causes of the fall of James II. " The whole army, and at last the people, both in city and country," declares Bishop Burnet, " were singing it perpetually, and," he adds, " perhaps never had so slight a thing so great an effect." Later on, Dr. Percy alleged that the words of *Lilliburlero* had more serious consequences than the philippics of Demosthenes or Cicero, and contributed largely towards bringing about the Revolution of 1688.

But whose idea was it to set the poem to Purcell's music? It was most probably that of the Puritan Lord Wharton (afterwards Lord-Lieutenant of Ireland in the reign of Queen Anne), who had constantly sat on the opposition benches in the House of Lords during the reigns of Charles II and James II. He boasted of having " sung a deluded king out of three kingdoms." His account of the matter is to be found in the third edition, published in 1712, of *A true relation of the several Facts and Circumstances of the intended Riot and Tumult on Queen Elizabeth's Birthday*. The " Quickstep " was reprinted in 1689 in a collection entitled *Musick's Handmaid for the Virginal or Harpsichord*, in which it is called " A new Irish tune."

Between the year 1680 and the accession of William III, the successor of James II, Purcell set his signature to ten dramatic works. In addition to *Theodosius, or the Force of Love*, mentioned above, and *The Virtuous Wife*, we may enumerate Shakspere's *King Richard II* (1681), adapted by Nahum Tate, performed under the name of *The Sicilian Usurper*, but stopped for political reasons after the first performance; *Sir Barnaby Whigg* (1681), a comedy by Tom d'Urfey; *The Double Marriage* (1682 or 1685), a tragedy by Beaumont and Fletcher; *The English Lawyer* (1683 or 1684), an adaptation by Edward Ravenscroft of a Latin comedy performed for the first time before James I in 1615; and *Circe* (1685), a tragedy by Charles Davenant. Downes states that the author had produced this tragedy between 1676 and 1681, with music by Banister. But as a matter of fact the information given by the author of the *Roscius Anglicanus* is inaccurate. We know that Tonson the publisher printed the piece and its incidental lyrics in 1677. It is very probable that the production of *Circe* took place at the same date; but it was not till its revival in 1685 that Purcell added the music. This music was wrongly attributed to Banister by Dr. Rimbault, but he frankly acknowledged his error in an article in *Concordia* for April 15–22, 1876. The style and quality of the music, and, what is more, some manuscripts of Purcell's, leave, in our opinion, not the slightest room for doubt as to the true identity of the composer.

In addition to the pieces enumerated above, we may mention *Sophonisba* (1685 or 1693), a tragedy by Nathaniel Lee, the subject of which is the defeat of Hannibal; *The Knight of Malta* (1686 or 1691) by Beaumont and Fletcher, and lastly a comedy by Tom d'Urfey, imitated from the same author's *The Noble Gentleman*. The hero of this piece is a simpleton who, having pushed himself forward at court, sees himself stripped of all the titles and honours conferred upon him in derision by practical jokers. The original piece was a favourite of Leigh Hunt's.

Among the religious works composed by Purcell during the period that we are now considering, we have already mentioned: *I was glad when they said unto me*, and *My heart is inditing*. Both of these are elaborately developed works, especially the latter, one of them occupying fifteen pages of the Purcell Society's edition, and the other fifty. Yet they form but a small portion of the works composed by Henry Purcell for performance in church. The verses of psalms set to music as anthems by the English master can be counted by scores. His autograph manuscripts are to be seen at the British Museum, Buckingham Palace, the Bodleian Library, Oxford, and the Fitzwilliam Museum, Cambridge. Perhaps the collection of anthems belonging to the Fitzwilliam Museum was started while Purcell was copyist to Westminster Abbey. The writing of the opening pages shows signs of a somewhat forced application — that of a conscientious professional scribe. The collection was intended to contain works by various authors; but gradually Purcell excluded from it all but his own. The anthems that it contains were most certainly composed for the Abbey. The index, drawn up by the author's own hand, is dated September 13, 1681. One curious detail may be noted: the collection begins at both ends. Both sides of the page have been used by the composer, and the book can be read from either end. There is also at Cambridge a collection of anthems by Purcell, transcribed by John Blow — a fresh proof of the friendship existing between

Blow and his famous pupil. This transcription dates from 1683.

The library of York Cathedral contains the anthem *Blow up the trumpet in Sion* (Joel ii. 1), which is not in Purcell's hand, but is certainly a work of his.

The Rev. J. Gostling had in his possession a collection of anthems dating from 1687 to 1688.

The anthem *They that go down to the sea in ships,* which has already been mentioned, owed its inspiration to the account of a storm at sea in which Charles II and the Duke of York were within an ace of perishing off the Kentish coast. The Rev. J. Gostling had been invited on board the King's yacht in order to contribute to the entertainment of the company, and he described the incident to Purcell, who, in order to commemorate it, composed this anthem, the words of which could not have been more appropriately chosen.

During the period between 1680 and 1689 — the second period of the musician's life — he was not spared his share of trials.

On July 31, 1682 he had the grief of losing his uncle Thomas, who before his death, however, had had the satisfaction of witnessing the successes of his nephew, to whom, as we have seen, he was tenderly attached. The two brothers, Henry senior and Thomas, lie side by side in the cloisters of Westminster Abbey.

His uncle Thomas had scarcely closed his eyes in death when a son was born to Henry Purcell. But the composer's joy was shortlived. The child, John Baptist, lived only a few months. Two other sons, christened one Thomas (1686), and the other Henry (1687), in memory of the dear ones whom he had lost, met with the same fate as little John Baptist. There was also a daughter Mary; but we have no precise information as to whether she too was prematurely snatched away by death.

Of the six children born to him, possibly three and certainly two survived him: Frances, born in 1688, and Edward, born in 1689.

In 1688 Purcell once more became copyist to Westminster Abbey. It is uncertain why he was once again called upon to occupy this post, and whether he solicited it — and if so, why. He occupied it for only two years.

The same year, 1688, witnessed the fall of James II. His son-in-law, the Stadtholder of Holland — who had saved his country by opening the sluices before the advancing army of Louis XIV — was proclaimed King of England under

the name of William III. The coronation ceremonies for King William and Queen Mary nearly
lost Purcell his place as organist to the Abbey. In
return for a money payment he admitted to
the organ-loft some persons desirous of having a
full view of the magnificent spectacle offered by
the ceremony. On April 18, 1689 he was ordered
to return the sums that he had charged, in accordance with a resolution passed by the Dean
and Chapter on March 25 previously, to the
effect that all moneys received for a place in
the Abbey, the organ-loft, or the adjoining
cemetery were to be paid over to the treasurer.
If Purcell refused to repay what he had received,
his appointment was to be declared null and void,
and part of his pay stopped. We have no precise
details as to how the dispute was settled. In the
treasurer's accounts for the year 1689 we find a
receipt for a lump sum in connexion with the
coronation festivities; moreover, these accounts
show that Purcell's salary was paid in full for
the whole year. Perhaps the organist returned
the sum he had received; perhaps a compromise
was arrived at to settle the affair. In any case the
minutes of the Chapter contain no allusion to
any further controversy.

This incident is related by Hawkins in a

manuscript note appended to his *History of Music,* and corroborated by one of his contemporaries, Dr. Benjamin Cooke. It is on record in two documents belonging to the Chapter of Westminster Abbey; in one of these documents, the minute-book of the Chapter, Purcell is alluded to as organist; in the other, the rough draft of these minutes, or else a copy of them, he is only called the organ-blower. Hawkins mistook this rough draft or copy of the minutes of the Chapter for the minutes themselves — that is to say, for the only genuine and authoritative document. Hawkins's error, which was only pointed out by Dr. Benjamin Cooke, in no wise affects the actual facts. It is merely a case of a verbal variation.

The year 1689 marks a fresh stage in Purcell's life. It is the starting-point of a period of even greater musical production — considerably greater, indeed. During the second period his composition for the theatre had not, on the whole, taken up much of the composer's time. During the third and last it absorbed all the leisure left him by the court, the town and the Church, not to speak of the composition of chamber music.

Following Mr. Barclay Squire, let us adopt

1689 as the year of publication of *Dido and Æneas*. This opera was to be the first of a fresh series of dramatic works, following closely one upon another, the number of which rose to upwards of fifty. Certain of these, such as *Amphitryon* (1690), adapted by Dryden from Molière's piece of that name, *The Female Vertuosos* (1693), an imitation by Thomas Wright of *Les Femmes savantes*, are signs of the wide prestige enjoyed by the great French comic dramatist in England at the end of the seventeenth century. *Amphitryon* is the first work in which Dryden's name is linked with that of Purcell. The poet, whose character was not on the same high level as his talent — which we may justly describe as genius — and who throughout his whole life was careful to trim his sails to every wind of court favour, had a few years previously called in the collaboration of Louis Grabu, who was in high repute at court, in transforming his play *Albion and Albanius* into an opera. " M. Grabu's qualities," he wrote, in the preface to the opera, " have raised him to a degree above any man who might pretend to be his rival on our stage." Grabu's music was an utter failure, performed only six times; whereas Purcell's *Dioclesian* had been received with approbation, though it had not been a financial success. Downes was to say of it later that this work " gratify'd the expectation of Court and City, and got the author great reputation." Mortified by the failure of the opera with the libretto of which he had furnished Louis Grabu, Dryden asked himself whether he might not be wise to get into touch with Purcell. He followed up this impulse and hastened to the aid of the already victorious composer. The published edition of *Amphitryon* is preceded by an Epistle Dedicatory, addressed to Sir William Leveson Gower, from which we quote the following remarks: " What has been wanting on my part has been abundantly supplyed by the Excellent Composition of Mr. *Purcell,* in whose Person we have at length found an *Englishman* equal with the best abroad." These details cast a somewhat unflattering light upon the character of John Dryden.

There were other dramatic works in which Purcell collaborated — for instance, Dryden's *King Arthur* (1691), and *Bonduca* (1695), adapted from a tragedy by Beaumont and Fletcher — which, like *Albion and Albanius,* are signs of a revival of national sentiment in the theatre. In *King Arthur* the poet represents the conflict between the Britons and Saxons. In

Bonduca we see the struggle between the Britons and Romans. The Britons are defeated, and their Queen, Bonduca, with her daughters, poisons herself in the presence of the Roman general.

Other pieces again, such as *The Indian Emperor* (1691) and *Aurengzebe*, were dramas in a style that Dryden was trying to acclimatize in England — the heroic style. Some — for instance, *Cleomenes*, a tragedy by Dryden and Lee (1692), *Pausanias* (1690), by one Norton, and *Regulus* (1692), by John Crowne — bear witness to the taste of the writer for subjects drawn from antiquity.

How many of these dramatic works, to which Purcell added the charm of his music, have survived? Very few indeed. A few names alone deserve to hold the attention of posterity: those of Dryden, Lee, a belated Elizabethan, Congreve, the writer of comedies, and perhaps Tom d'Urfey, on account of his lively humour. Dryden's dramatic works are adorned with many a graceful passage — witness the following, drawn from *King Arthur:*

> Fairest Isle, all Isles excelling,
> Seat of pleasure and of Love!
> Venus here will choose her dwelling
> And forsake her Cyprian grove.

Cupid from his fav'rite nation
Care and Envy will remove;
Jealousy that poisons Passion
And Despair that dies for Love.

Gentle murmurs, sweet complaining,
Sighs that blow the fire of Love,
Soft repulses, kind disdaining
Shall be all the pains you prove.

Ev'ry swain shall pay his duty,
Grateful ev'ry nymph shall prove,
And as these excel in beauty,
Those shall be renown'd for love.

This pearl among islands, as will easily be guessed, is none other than Great Britain.

Certain of Dryden's dramatic works are of an elevated character — for instance *Aureng-zebe*. The nobility of feeling displayed by the leading character, Aurengzebe, commands our admiration, but does not stir us deeply. " Corneille had indeed founded the tragic style upon admiration," say MM. Cazamian and Legouis, apropos of Dryden in their *Histoire de la littérature anglaise*. But, they add, " if the Cornelian hero merits our entire sympathy, it is because his nobility is a victory, gained at the price of a cruel struggle with himself. In Dryden the

conception of heroism is lacking in all this sub-
tlety and, it must be said, in all this idealism."
Whatever may be the merits of this poet's dramatic works, they would never have made his
name famous for all time. It is as a satirist that
he has earned immortality.

The Restoration dramatists often seemed
to take a wilful pleasure in spoiling the subjects
that they had chosen. Thus in the tragedy
which he founded upon Mrs. Aphra Behn's fine
romance *Oroonoko,* the subject of which is a
prince reduced to slavery, Thomas Southerne invented comic episodes that have not the slightest
connexion with the tragedy itself; and under
the title of *Dioclesian,* Betterton produced a
mangled version of Beaumont and Fletcher's
Prophetess.

What the public demanded above all at the
Restoration period were dazzling spectacular effects. In giving an account of a performance
Downes hardly mentions anything but the splendour of the costumes, the beauty of the stage
setting, and the degree of perfection attained by
mechanical devices. The work itself is relegated
to the background. The contemporaries of
Charles II were filled with wonder when the
witches in Sir William Davenant's adaptation

of *Macbeth* flew off into the air; or when, in *Theodosius,* a blood-stained cross, surrounded by angels, with the words *In hoc signo vinces,* appeared at the back of the stage before the kneeling Constantine.

There can be no doubt that, by creating a suitable atmosphere around the chief characters, the stage setting heightens the spectator's satisfaction and emotion; and it would be childish to deny its utility. But it ought always to be the handmaiden of dramatic art; whereas throughout the whole Restoration period it claimed to treat the drama as a mere slave. The dramatists of that age did not consider that the works of Shakspere or Beaumont and Fletcher lent themselves to the scenic effects beloved of the public; and this is why they adapted them. By the additions and mutilations to which they subjected them they distorted their very spirit and impaired their significance, even when they did not completely destroy it. " Even Dryden himself," say MM. Cazamian and Legouis, " calmly lent his hand to this profanation," in spite of his respect for " the sacred name of Shakspere."

The greatest literary sinner of the age was Thomas Shadwell, whom Dryden lashed with his satire in *Absalom and Achitophel:*

The midwife laid her hand on his thick skull
With this prophetic blessing: Be thou dull!

Southey placed Shadwell in the lowest rank of the hierarchy of poets laureate; while the opinion of him expressed by Lord Rochester was: " If Shadwell were to burn all he has written, and print all he has said, he would have more wit and humour than any other poet." It must be admitted, then, that Shadwell could claim the merit of being a brilliant talker.

But, not content with laying sacrilegious hands upon the structure of the works that he presented to the public (in Shakspere's *Timon of Athens*, for instance, he suppressed twenty of the characters, and created eleven new ones of his own devising), he went further, and played havoc with the poetic diction of the original. It may interest our readers if we place a specimen of Shadwell's text side by side with that of Shakspere.

At the conclusion of the masque, Shakspere puts the following words into Timon's mouth:

You have done our pleasures much grace, fair ladies,
Set a fair fashion on our entertainment,
Which was not half so beautiful and kind;

86

You have added worth unto 't, and lustre,
And entertain'd me with mine own device;
I am to thank you for it.

Now let us turn to Shadwell's version:

'Tis well design'd and well perform'd, and I'll
Reward you well; let us retire into my next
Apartment, where I've devised new pleasures for you;
And where I will distribute some small presents
To testifie my Love and Gratitude.

How striking is the contrast between the chivalrous courtesy of Shakspere's Timon and the meanness and ostentation of Shadwell's. Moreover, the metrical qualities of these two extracts differ as widely as the thoughts which they express, the verse of the former being as well-knit as that of the latter is invertebrate.

The purpose of these remarks upon the character of drama during the Restoration period is simply to show that Purcell often lavished the treasures of his genius on a most worthless object. How few of the writers with whom he collaborated still live in the memory of posterity! The inferiority of most of the works to which Purcell's music was the fairest ornament is so great that they are no longer acted; a circumstance from which the composer's reputation suffers, though it cannot detract from his artistic merit. *Dioclesian* has no value save that of the music in which it is interpreted. Though the libretto of *King Arthur* is from Dryden's pen, it is very inferior to the general run of that writer's works. And what we have said of *Dioclesian* and *King Arthur* applies to a host of other plays.

The scope allowed to music in the dramatic works to which Purcell has set his name varies greatly. *The English Lawyer* contains only one piece, a rollicking three-part catch entitled " My wife has a tongue! " *King Richard II* has an air with three verses: " Retired from any mortal's sight "; *Sir Barnaby Whigg,* a duet for tenor or soprano and bass: " Blow, Boreas, blow "; *Sophonisba,* one soprano air only: " Beneath the poplar's shadow "; *The Knight of Malta* merely a single catch: " At the close of the Evening." *Theodosius* contains eight musical numbers; *The Double Marriage,* nine; the music of *A Fool's Preferment* fills twelve pages of the Purcell Society's edition; that of *The Virtuous Wife* fourteen; and that of *Circe* twenty-five. The incidental music for *King Arthur, Dioclesian, The Indian Queen,* and *The Fairy Queen* respectively attains the proportions of a fair-sized

opera; and though more restricted in *Bonduca,*
The Tempest, Timon, and *Don Quixote,* it is
still of imposing dimensions.

But, in spite of appearances, the theatre was
far from monopolizing Purcell's attention. As a
matter of fact his activity was equally unflagging
in other spheres.

On August 5, 1689 he produced his ode,
Celestial Music, composed in honour of the return of the Prince of Denmark.

Every year the leading residents of Yorkshire — as, indeed, of other counties — used to
meet together at a banquet, after attending divine service, " not only to promote Good Fel-
lowship, but also to cultivate the sacred claims
of Charity and Benevolence " — to quote Dr.
Cummings. It was for such an occasion that Purcell composed his fine ode known as *The Yorkshire Feast Song,* which was performed in the
Merchant Taylors' Hall. The cost of production
amounted to a hundred pounds, an enormous
sum at that period.

Between 1689 and 1694 he composed six
odes to celebrate Queen Mary's birthday, the
date of which was April 30. The first: *Now does
the glorious day appear,* was performed at Whitehall " before Their Majesties." The words were

composed by Shadwell, and contain allusions to the fear inspired by William III in " the trembling Papal world."

The second extols the King's military prowess. By the time the third was performed, the King was in Flanders, at war with Louis XIV. The French army had just won a victory, and the town of Mons had fallen into the hands of the King of France. The author of the words for the third ode expresses his conviction that God will bless his " godlike son," and crown the efforts of the English fleet and army with success, while the Queen administers with wisdom the kingdom defended by the sovereign.

The fourth ode, *Love's Goddess sure is blind,* the fifth, *Celebrate this festival,* to words by Nahum Tate, and lastly the sixth, *Ye sons of Art,* exalt the sovereign's virtues.

The words of the fourth are particularly elegant, being the work of Sir Charles Sedley, the courtier-poet, whose morals were as corrupt as his literary taste was refined. This ode contains one song, " May her blest example chase," the bass of which is, note for note, the air of an old Scottish ballad, " Cold and Raw." According to Hawkins, this air was introduced into the ode as follows: Queen Mary had been listening to a number of Purcell's pieces performed by Mrs. Arabella Hunt and accompanied on the harpsichord by the composer himself. After a while the sovereign desired Mrs. Hunt to sing the Scottish ballad, and Mrs. Hunt naturally responded to the royal command, accompanying herself on the lute. Purcell, who was not performing, witnessed the Queen's satisfaction and was a little chagrined to find a popular ballad preferred to his own music. He concealed his feelings, but determined to introduce the air into the next ode which he should compose in honour of the Queen. Cummings considers that this anecdote is probably authentic. Purcell could certainly have found no more graceful way of expressing his disappointment.

These six odes form a magnificent tribute to the sovereign to whom they were dedicated, and their official character in no way detracts from their sincerity. In declaring that the death of Queen Mary was " extremely lamented," Dr. Tudway was merely voicing the feelings of the public. Queen Mary had managed to win the hearts of all her subjects. Her funeral, which took place on March 5, 1695, is described by contemporaries in touching terms. No less than thirty-six odes or monodies in commemoration of her bounty were composed by musicians of the day, among whom should be mentioned John Blow. Two anthems by Purcell, *Blessed is the man that feareth the Lord*, and *Thou knowest, Lord*, were performed at Westminster Abbey during the funeral ceremony, the second of which was specially composed for the occasion, and was the last piece of sacred music bearing Purcell's signature. Two pieces by him are included among the thirty-six odes or monodies which we mentioned above; one for the solo voice, *Incassum, Lesbia*, the other for two voices, *O dive custos auriacæ domus*. All these tributes to the late Queen were apparently deserved, but Shadwell was going to rather excessive lengths when he wrote in the words for the ode of 1689:

No more shall we the great Eliza boast,
For her great name in greater Mary's will be lost.

During this last period of his life, Purcell did not cease to compose new anthems.

In 1695 his position in the musical world made it incumbent upon him to sing the praises of a six-year-old child, son of the princess who afterwards became Queen Anne, the Duke of Gloucester, a poor, sickly child, who died in 1700, at the age of eleven.

St. Cecilia continued to be an object of veneration to Purcell, and he wrote two new odes or cantatas in her honour. That of 1692, the words of which were composed by Nicholas Brady, who collaborated with Nahum Tate in the metrical version of the Psalms, in a work imposing alike in its æsthetic value and in its dimensions. To Purcell's devotion to the patron saint of musicians we also owe the *Te Deum* and *Jubilate* in D (1694), which may be regarded as his masterpiece, or at any rate as one of his masterpieces, and which met with an enormous success, being performed on St. Cecilia's day every year from 1697 to 1713; while between 1713 and 1743 it was performed alternately with the *Te Deum* and *Jubilate* composed by Handel to celebrate the Peace of Utrecht.

There were yet other works of Purcell's which we have not mentioned: the Latin anthems *Jehovah, quam multi sunt hostes* and *Beati omnes qui timent Dominum*; besides certain pieces of a religious character, a *Laudate Dominum* for three voices in canon, a *Gloria Patri* in G minor for four voices, the scheme of which consists in a double canon, in which the second part is the first one reversed; and an *Alleluia*, also for four voices, which reads as a canon *recte et retro*, as explained below. This *Alleluia* is written for two counter-tenors and two basses. The first counter-tenor part is read normally, from left to right, the second from right to left, beginning at the end, and exactly reproducing the first. The bass parts are read in exactly the same way, one forwards and the other backwards. The Flemings excelled in *tours de force* of this kind, which were in great vogue in the sixteenth century, though they are somewhat futile; for it is impossible to follow the contrary movement of the parts by ear alone; at any rate it is only exceptionally gifted musicians who can cope with them. Byrd wrote a canon for eight voices, *recte et retro*. " It is hardly possible to study this complication attentively," says Grove, " without feeling one's brain turn giddy; and yet, strange to say, the effect produced is less curious than beautiful."

We have still to mention a second collection of sonatas, which was published after Purcell's death, by his widow. This collection contains ten sonatas for two violins, bass, and harpsichord. They differ but little from those of the previous collection, consisting, like them, of slow and quick movements in alternation. Strictly speaking, they are suites rather than sonatas; they consist of a series of movements each embodying a poetical theme (or idea), which is not formally developed. The time had not yet come when the sonata was to be based upon two distinct musical themes, developed according to strict rules.

We may also mention among Purcell's works a sonata in G minor for violin and harpsichord, eight suites, some minuets, preludes, gavottes, and grounds, a chaconne, a toccata in A, four pieces for the organ, etc. Certain of his pieces were published during his lifetime by Playford in the second part of the collection entitled *Musick's Handmaid;* the rest did not appear till after his death, when they were published by Mrs. Purcell.

The composer is also to be credited with a number of catches, rounds, and two- or three-part songs, which form the twenty-second volume of the Purcell Society's edition. These catches were sung at table in the presence of Charles II, James II, and William III. Many are drinking-songs, usually in three parts. The words of some of them are quite decorous, and appear in collections for schools. Others are somewhat licentious; but all of them are full of jollity. The English have always displayed a marked preference for catches, especially at the Restoration period. A great number were written by Henry Hall, John Blow, George Day (organist of Wimborne, Dorset), Tudway, and John Eccles (who became master of the Royal Band on the death of Nicholas Staggins). The two- and three-part songs are for the most part sentimental, and some of them are elaborately developed. The song " See where she sits weeping," the words of which are by Abraham Cowley, is a small cantata, the voices being accompanied by violins and a bass (a violoncello *ad libitum*). It was Mr. Barclay Squire's task to edit the catches and rounds, of which there are fifty-seven in existence; and Mr. Fuller-Maitland's to edit the two- and three-part songs, of which there are forty-seven. This was no easy matter; for many of these pieces appeared in the *Pleasant Musical Companion;* and a number of others came out in a variety of obscure publications.

We should also be careful not to forget twenty or so fantasias, the manuscripts of which are in the British Museum, and ten of which have recently been transcribed by Mr. Peter Warlock, edited by M. André Mangeot, and published by Messrs. J. Curwen and Son. We may also mention some anthems in Purcell's handwriting which are, alas, unfinished: *Lord, not to us; Ah!*

few and full of sorrow are the dayes of Man;
Hear me, O Lord, and that soon, etc. The study
which we have made of these in the Department
of Manuscripts at the British Museum explains
our regret; for these anthems, incomplete as they
are, bear the stamp of the master's genius.

Will it ever be possible to draw up a complete catalogue of Purcell's works? Many have
been lost through lapse of time. Perhaps there
are some in existence which are still unknown.
Perhaps more will be discovered in the penetralia
of some English or continental library. The Bib-
liothèque Sainte-Geneviève in Paris, for instance,
possesses a manuscript rondo in three parts, bearing the name of Purcell. Unfortunately there is
no Christian name on the document, the catalogue giving the name as " Daniel or Henry "
(I, 499, nos. 1097–8). The words have the true
seventeenth-century flavour:

> Cupids, strew your paths with flowers
> Gathered from Elysian bowers.

The music does not, in our opinion, furnish
any conclusive indications of its authorship;
for Daniel often — indeed, always — imitated
Henry. But the rondo bears a characteristic stamp
of elegance which justifies us in attributing it to

the elder brother. It is by studying the hand-writing of the document that we are best able to trace its origin; and as a matter of fact there is a strong resemblance between the hand in which both words and music are written and the manu-scripts of Henry Purcell. Our impression is that the rondo is really from the pen of the greater of the two composers.

The number of works by Henry Purcell handed down to posterity is indeed stupendous. It matters little that the same themes sometimes occur in two different works. For instance, the charming air " There's not a swain," from *Rule a wife and have a wife,* forms the theme of the first hornpipe in *The Fairy Queen.* The only dif-ference is that the air is in E minor and the horn-pipe in G minor. The overture to the masque in *Timon of Athens* is almost identical with the sonata known as the Trumpet Sonata. The over-ture to the ode *Celebrate this Festival,* dedicated to Queen Mary, is the same as the overture to the ode to St. Cecilia of 1692, the sole distinction be-ing that the former is in C and the latter in D. The number of Purcell's works is all the more amazing because he died so young. At the age of thirty-seven his career was abruptly cut short by consumption, and he expired on November

21, 1695, on the very eve of the Feast of St. Cecilia, which had inspired him with those works in which fervent emotion is combined with musical science. His end was obviously hastened by overwork. During the year 1695 he was forced to take John Eccles into collaboration in order to finish his *Don Quixote*. He never finished his *Indian Queen,* the completion of which was entrusted to Daniel. The younger brother's contribution is not very extensive, being confined to one act, styled an " Additional Act "; but it is enough to throw the difference between the styles of the two brothers into striking relief. At first sight they present very much the same appearance; but we do not need to indulge in a lengthy examination of the musical text before arriving at the conclusion that the one is as varied, picturesque, and daring as the other is, on the whole, monotonous, undistinguished, and hesitating. Those of our readers desirous of carrying the comparison between the musical idiom of the two brothers further may turn to the *Magnificat* which each of them composed. Daniel's *Magnificat* does not venture out of the keys of B minor and G minor, and shows but small trace of any affinity between the words and the music. Its tone is uniformly plaintive — for no apparent reason; for the words of the canticle are not at all melancholy.

Henry Purcell saw his end approaching and, with the shadow of death gathering close around him, found strength to draw up his will on the very day when he breathed his last.

The scene of Purcell's death, like that of his birth, has been the subject of much controversy. Did he pass away only a few steps from Westminster Abbey, in a house on the west side of Dean's Yard, while a service was in progress? Was he ushered into eternity by the solemn tones of the organ, still, perhaps, perceptible to his ear, even during his death-agony? Dr. Cummings alleges that such was the case, and his assertion is to a certain extent corroborated by the fact that, in announcing the third edition of her late husband's *Lessons for the Harpsichord* in 1696, Mrs. Purcell gives as her address a house in Dean's Yard. Sir Frederick Bridge followed up Cummings's investigations into this question, which interested him both as a musical historian and as organist to the Abbey. The result of his inquiries, which he published in the *Musical Times* for November 1895 (p. 734), was to establish the following facts: Mrs. Purcell's name does not appear on the Rate-book for 1696–7 as occupier of any house in Dean's Yard, part of which lies within the parish of St. Margaret's, Westminster, and part within the precincts of the Abbey. Moreover, the Rev. H. F. Westlake informed the writer that in the archives of the Abbey — which exist intact from the year 1660 onwards — there is no mention of any residence within the Abbey precincts as having been rented in the name of Henry or Mrs. Purcell. There was indeed a house known as Purcell House in existence fifteen years ago on the west side of Dean's Yard; but this house was built after the musician's death. On the other hand, there is a record of rates for 1695–6 paid by Mrs. Purcell as occupier of a residence in Marsham Street, Westminster. Sir Frederick Bridge's conclusion — to which the Rev. H. F. Westlake also inclined — is that Purcell died in Marsham Street. There are evidently some grounds for stripping the actual facts of the poetic setting devised by Dr. Cummings.

We have four excellent portraits of Henry Purcell, one by Kneller, and three others by Clostermann. The last portrait dates from the very year of his death. Beneath the likeness of the composer is the coat of arms described above, and below that, again, his Christian name and surname in Latin; while the inscription "*Ætat. Suæ* 37 —

95 " is printed under the name. This piece of evidence has served as an additional justification for fixing the date of Purcell's birth in the year 1658.

We cannot fail to submit to our readers a short account of the circumstances that brought about Purcell's death, as related by Sir John Hawkins. " There is a tradition," says Sir John, " that his death was occasioned by a cold which he caught in the night, waiting for admittance into his own house. It is said that he used to keep late hours, and that his wife had given orders to his servants not to let him in after midnight! Unfortunately he came home heated with wine from the tavern at an hour later than that prescribed him, and through the inclemency of the air he contracted a disorder of which he died. If this be true, it reflects but little honour on Madam Purcell, for so she is styled in the advertisements of his works."

This account given by Hawkins is not based upon any clear or definite evidence, but upon a tradition, of which he omits to state the source, and which he accepts with light-hearted negligence, merely repeating a piece of gossip, upon which he proceeds to base his insinuations.

In his will Purcell twice alludes to Mrs. Purcell as a " loving wife." Possibly he may have done so out of pride or weakness; but the fact remains that he left her all his property. For her own part, in publishing a great number of his works Mrs. Purcell never omitted to pay a tribute to his memory. In dedicating the *Orpheus Britannicus* to Lady Howard, she speaks of him in the most touching terms, referring to him as her " dear " and " lamented " husband in a way that leaves us no doubt as to her real feelings.

At a later date Lady Hawkins was exposed to ill-natured comments with regard to her attitude towards Sir John. Her daughter undertook her defence, and declared in her *Anecdotes, Biographical Sketches* that the accusations made against Mrs. Purcell might be as gross calumnies as those directed against her own mother. It is possible to read into this statement a delicate and perfectly filial repudiation of her father's insinuations against the composer and his wife.

The joviality of Purcell's character found ready expression. His catches, indeed, bear witness to it. He enjoyed life, but there is no documentary evidence, nor is there any testimony on the part of his contemporaries, representing him as of loose morals. He was frequently obliged to return home late as a result of his profession. So far as we know, he remained uncontaminated by the moral corruption of which he had repeated occasion to observe the effects from his youth upwards. The reader will recall the brief account that we have given of the morals of the Restoration period.

At what conclusion, then, was Hawkins trying to arrive? At the end of the remarks quoted above we read the following sentence: " It seems probable that the disease of which [Purcell] died was rather a lingering than an acute one, perhaps a consumption." Was it only in order to lead up to such a conclusion that he went out of his way, as it seems, to blacken the memory of the musician and his wife? Boswell was quite right to add a note in his *Life of Johnson,* to the effect that " Sir John's carelessness to ascertain facts is very remarkable." Indeed, Hawkins's *History of Music* contains a large number of serious errors, and his assertions must be received with caution. We should accept as genuine only those of the anecdotes related by him which are also recorded by other writers, or else seem highly probable. For instance, Hawkins alleges that " It is said that Dryden wrote his *Alexander's Feast* with a view to its being set to music by Purcell; but that Purcell declined the task, as thinking it beyond the

power of music to express sentiments so super-
latively energetic as that ode abounds with."
Yet Dryden's ode was written two years after the
musician's death!

Henry Purcell was survived by his sister
Katherine, who had married the Rev. William
Sale of Sheldwich, Kent, and by his mother,
whose death, in 1699, is recorded in the registers
of St. Margaret's, Westminster. Nothing has been
said of them in this work, for they do not seem
to have exercised any real influence on the musician's destiny. We may, however, remark that
Purcell's mother was with her daughter-in-law
and grandchildren when her son breathed his
last. The reader will no doubt remember that at
least two, and possibly three, of his children survived their father. Frances, who on the death of
her mother, in 1706, became her executrix and
sole heiress, married the poet Leonard Welstead
at the age of nineteen, and ended her days in
1724, at the age of thirty-six. As we may see,
the Purcell family suffered more than once from
the ravages of premature death.

Edward followed the career of his father, being organist first of St. Clement's, Eastcheap, and
afterwards of St. Margaret's, Westminster, and
died in 1740. He was a praiseworthy musician,

but no more, and would certainly not have succeeded in making a great name by his own efforts. And yet on his death-bed his father expressly desired Mrs. Purcell to see that the child received a good musical training. His mother brought the child up with the most tender and devoted care. On her death-bed she confided him to the care of Frances, who as heiress to her property had to take charge of him until he was in a position to earn his living. At the same time by a nuncupatory testament — that is, one consisting in an oral declaration — she bestowed upon Edward all the music-books that had belonged to the composer or herself, besides an organ, two spinets, a silver tankard, a silver watch, two pairs of gold buttons, a hair-ring, a mourning-ring, a " larum clock," " Mr. Edward Purcell's picture," and a handsome set of bedroom furniture. These details seem to us of some importance, for they would seem to show that in all probability Mrs. Purcell was not in straitened circumstances at her death, or on the death of her husband. She would surely not have kept the organ and the two spinets if she had been in a destitute condition. Unfortunately there is no conclusive evidence extant with regard to her material position; but, without venturing on any rash allegations, we are justified in supposing that Henry Purcell had gradually risen by his own personal efforts and energy — not to speak of his genius — to what is vulgarly known as a good position. Fine feathers do not make fine birds, says the proverb, and often this is true. But the portraits painted by Clostermann represent Purcell as wearing fine lace ruffles, an impeccably cut gown, and silk breeches. And it is hardly to be supposed that the artist would embellish his sitter beyond all recognition!

IV

The Works of Henry Purcell

1. Purcell's Debt to Lully

THROUGH PELHAM HUMPHREY PURCELL obtained the benefit of the experience that the former had gained on the Continent.

The influence of Lully upon Purcell is undeniable. But must we therefore conclude that he lacks originality? If so, then the same charge might be brought against Lully, for he owes a great deal to contemporary musicians and those who lived just before him. In both his religious and his secular works Purcell, like the Florentine master, opens with a symphony, immediately followed by a piece in fugue style, these two pieces forming the overture. To grasp this point we need only glance at the odes, anthems, or dramatic works. The 3/4 time which Purcell so frequently uses is akin to the dance rhythms that are so common in Lully. But the superintendent of Louis XIV's music had modelled himself in turn upon Cavalli.

M. Romain Rolland remarks on this subject: " The structure of Cavalli's *Ercole* has many points of resemblance with that of Lully's operas at a later date: among these are the important part played by the *sinfonie*, the fugal style of the overture, with its spirited and abrupt rhythms, the construction of the prologue, the choruses and dances in which the acts end, the songs sung to a dance rhythm. . . . All the same, it must be recognized that in this work even Cavalli was adapting himself to the taste prevailing in France at the time." " Lully," says Monsieur Rolland again, " did not invent either the minuet, the gavotte or the bourrée, which were dances of French origin and had attained their complete development before his time."

As a matter of fact there were a large number of dances known in Italy at the time of the *Sacre Rappresentazioni* in which they formed part of the program. But in France too the dance followed a spontaneous and normal course of development. It had an independent existence and was always in favour at court. Does not Froissart tell us that at the marriage of a Chevalier du Vermandois with one of the Queen's ladies in 1392 (old style) there was dancing at the Hôtel Saint-Pol, where " there was mikel goodly company and noble lords "? The festivities were cut short by a " grievious mishap (*dolente aventure*)." The costumes of the young nobles disguised as savages caught fire, as the result of an imprudence. Everybody has heard of the *Balet Comique de la Royne* of which Henri III's court was the scene on the occasion of the marriage of the Duc de Joyeuse with Marguerite de Lorraine-Vaudémont in 1582. Everybody knows, too, that Louis XIII and Louis XIV did not think it derogatory to them to take part in the court ballets. What conclusion, then, are we to draw from the lines of M. Romain Rolland's quoted above, except that Lully merely inherited a tradition, which he exploited to wonderful advantage?

There was one style — the pastoral — which

was in high favour throughout the whole of the seventeenth century, and to which Purcell, like Lully, was greatly addicted. But Lully had had famous precursors: Cavalli, Monteverde, Cesti, not to mention Cambert, whose *Les Peines et les Plaisirs de l'Amour* and *Pomone* are true pastorals. Like Lully, Purcell often had recourse to a vertical style of writing, in which each note of the melody is supported by a chord; and that not only in graceful choruses, such as " How blest are shepherds, how happy their lasses," from *King Arthur,* but in those vocal ensembles in which he attempts with signal success to obtain a massive body of sound — for instance, in " Praise the Lord, O Jerusalem " from *My heart is inditing*. But the vertical style was not invented by Lully; it had come into existence side side with the monodic style.

Like Lully again, Purcell sometimes doubles the voice part in the bass of his harmony. This will be seen if we compare the solo of the Cold Genius, " Great Love, I know thee now," in *King Arthur,* with the famous air " *L'Amour meurt dans mon cœur* " from Lully's *Persée*. But Cambert had already used this device in the air of the Faun " *Apollon pour Climène ne fait que soupirer* " from *Les Peines et les Plaisirs de*

l'Amour (Scene V), and in the air of the Faun
" *Voilà le prix de vos musiques* " from *Pomone*
(Scene VI).

Like Lully, Purcell used the utmost care in
his treatment of lyrical declamation; but while,
to quote M. Romain Rolland again, " Lully's
recitative " — and, we would add, his airs too —
" closely follow the movement of the words, and
are modelled on the verse "; while " the first rule
with him is the strict observance of the syllabic
style," Purcell enters more deeply into the meaning of the words and interprets it in the music;
he does not merely take the number of feet in the
verse as his guide. Consequently, in the work of
the Florentine master, as indeed in that of Cambert and of Luigi Rossi, there are incessant variations of rhythm; whereas in the work of the
English composer the rhythm remains regular.
Lully was not the first who resorted to every device of musical expression in order to make his
music a faithful mirror of the literary text. His
Italian predecessors, not to speak of Heinrich
Schütz, known as " the father of German music "
(1585–1672), had succeeded in bringing out the
significance of the words in the music. The advice which H. Schütz gave to singers, as long ago
as 1619, is expressed in the following picturesque

terms: " If they do not pronounce the words in a distinct and comprehensible manner, the music will be no more than a battle of flies, thereby defeating the intention of the composer."

Following the example of Lully, Cavalli, Luigi Rossi, etc., Purcell makes great use of a rhythmic figure based on a succession of dotted quavers followed by semi-quavers, ♪ ♪ , to express gaiety or violent emotion; but this form of expression had frequently been employed by Cesti, Monteverde, and Frescobaldi before him. The French organist Gigault, one of the presumed masters of Lully, was somewhat belated when he wrote: " It is also possible to make the movement more animated by using dotted notes at will."

Henry Purcell, like Captain Cooke's pupils in general, not to speak of all the English composers of the Restoration period, very often made use, in slow movements, of the 3/2 bar dear to many Italian musicians such as Cesti, Carissimi, and Cavalli. The same can be said of the rhythm in 3/4 and 6/4 time, based on the coincidence of the accented beat with a crotchet followed by a minim ‖ ♪ ♪ ‖ ♪ ♪ ♪ ‖· Purcell, above all, had a particular affection for this rhythm.

Needless to say, Purcell was conversant with

everything that went on in the musical world
during the Restoration period. The teaching of
his masters, his studies, his individual observa-
tions, the performances of the French and Italian
opera, for the establishment of which Hortense
Mancini, Duchesse de Mazarin, had provided the
money, the collections of Italian airs published by
Godbid and J. Playford in 1679, had all made
him familiar with the musical output of his day
and of the preceding age. If we refuse to con-
cede any originality to H. Purcell, on the grounds
that he borrowed certain forms of musical expression from Lully, as well as from various
Italian masters and perhaps some German ones, it
is only logical to refuse that quality to Handel
also. Indeed, in neither his secular nor his religious
writings has Handel greatly modified the system adopted by his predecessors. Almost all his
works open with a symphony followed by a
fugue. Like Purcell he wrote sonatas for two
violins and harpsichord. As in Purcell, quick
movements alternate with slow ones: the opening Adagio leads to a piece in fugal style which
recalls the Canzona of the English composer, followed by a Largo or Larghetto and a rapid Fi-
nale. So far as the arrangement of the movements
is concerned, the Handelian sonata is almost ex-

actly modelled upon that of Corelli — for instance, the rhythmic texture of many of Handel's finest pages consists of series of dotted quavers followed by semi-quavers. The times that he uses are those of the old musicians. And does not J. S. Bach, the greatest master of all, owe much to H. Schütz, to Pachelbel, to Buxtehude, Lotti, and Vivaldi? Does not the overture to his Suite in D major correspond to the work of the French type of which Lully is a brilliant example? The very names of the pieces that make up this suite are enough to reveal French influence: Aria, Gavotte, Bourrée, Gigue. . . . We may see to what absurdities we are inevitably led if we consider nothing but the outward form of works of art.

Like nature, art does not proceed by abrupt transitions. Lully, like Purcell, inherited from his predecessors the forms in which he cast his ideas, but these ideas bore the stamp of his own personality. The symphonies of the Florentine composer are of a solemn, massive, and majestic character, unknown before his day. Cambert had worked in the burlesque style. Both interest and pleasure are to be found in studying the Italian trio that closes the score of *Les Peines et les Plaisirs de l'Amour*. But if we compare this trio with the slave scene in *Le Sicilien,* on the words " *Chiribirida ouch alla, star bonturca, non aver danara,*" or with the third *divertissement* in *M. de Pourceaugnac,* to the words " *La polygamie est un cas pendable,*" we shall quickly see that Lully's comic passages have greater breadth and a more genuine *vis comica.* It is true that Lully had as his librettist not Gilbert, but Molière; but it is also true that in collaboration with such a partner he might well have proved quite unworthy of his task.

Under his almost magic baton the ballets underwent a complete change. " He conducted them at a quick pace," according to M. Romain Rolland, " and had a marked preference for lively and sharply accented numbers, such as the gigue (jig), canari (' canaries '), or forlane (*forlana*) ."

In the composition of his ballet music, as well as in conducting it, Lully displayed a characteristically Italian animation and verve. As regards the pastoral style, M. Romain Rolland says again: " In this sphere nobody could compare with him. This insensible, superficial soul, with more intelligence than true feeling, achieved a sincerity and purity of emotion in the pastoral manner that place him on a level with the most poetic among composers. There is scarcely an opera of his that is not instinct with this poetry of nature, night, and silence."

In short, neither opera, symphony, nor musical composition was created in a day. The artist enriches the heritage handed down to him with all the resources of his individual genius. The same is true of architecture. Style succeeds style, each preserving certain features from the preceding age and including elements which, from being merely accessory, become fully developed in the age that follows. For instance, the earliest examples of the Gothic style still preserve the austerity of the Romanesque. Or again the church of Saint-Eustache is in the Renaissance style, but it still bears numerous traces of Gothic art. Or take the château of Azay-le-Rideau: it, too, belongs to the Renaissance style, yet its general appearance is mediæval. The torch of art is passed on from hand to hand. It is at once the artist's task and glory to pursue his development towards an ideal that is constantly renewed, the elements of which are already present in those who have gone before him.

The imposing dimensions of Henry Purcell's works cause the commentator some qualms. Indeed, we hesitate before pointing out any particular work rather than another as typical of the English master's creative faculties. We must confine ourselves to mentioning certain pieces only which seem to us particularly characteristic. The reader will have no difficulty in finding others that are hardly less typical, or perhaps equally so, if he cares to approach the study of Purcell for himself.

2.

The Original and Personal Element in Purcell's Work

VARIETY is the first point that strikes us in Purcell's genius. Our moral sentiments and emotions invariably meet with a faithful rendering at his hands, and wide indeed is the field that they cover. He overflows with wit of the liveliest description in the scene of *The Fairy Queen* (P. S. Ed., XII, 21) where the drunken poet invites the fairies to play at blind-man's-buff. The whole scene trips in quavers and semi-quavers, which accentuate the monosyllabic character of the text.

The fantastic note prevails in the duet " Behold the man," from *The Richmond Heiress* (P. S. Ed., XXI, 53).

Fantasy and humour are blended in the tenor air " I'll sail upon the dog-star " (P. S. Ed.,

AUTOGRAPH PASSAGE FROM *The Fairy Queen*

AUTOGRAPH PASSAGE FROM *The Fairy Queen*

XX, 17), from *A Fool's Preferment*," the words of which are extremely curious:

> I'll sail upon the dog-star
> And then pursue the morning.
>   I'll chase the moon
>   Till it be noon;
> But I'll make her leave her horning.
>
> I'll climb the frosty morning
> And there I'll coin the weather.
> I'll tear the Rainbow from the sky
> And tye both ends together.
>
> The stars pluck from their orbs too
> And crowd them in my budget.
> And whether I'm a roaring boy,
> Let all the nation judge it.

Purcell's music, with its combination of pomposity and jollity, admirably renders the presumptuous frivolity of Tom d'Urfey's Fool.

The grace and elegance of his music are illustrated by the chorus from *King Arthur*, " How blest are shepherds, how happy their lasses "; by Psalm civ. 19, " He appointed the moon for seasons "; and by all the ballet airs, minuets, bourrées, rondos, gavottes, jigs, hornpipes, etc., especially those from *The Fairy Queen* and *Bonduca*.

Its sprightly lightness by: " Come unto these yellow sands," from *The Tempest*.

Its robust alertness and freshness by " Full fathom five " (these last two songs are sung by Ariel; in the one is mirrored his aerial elusiveness, in the other his healthy moral vigour).

Its good humour by " Nymphs and shepherds," from *The Libertine,* and the second air from *The Indian Queen* (P. S. Ed., XIX, 2).

Its nobility, not without a touch of pomp, by Ismeron the magician's air " By the croaking of the toad," from *The Indian Queen.*

Its sprightliness by the finales of the sonatas, the psalms " Clap your hands, O ye hills " and " Rejoice in the Lord alway," and the " Alleluias " of the anthems, notably that leading up to the anthem *Unto Thee will I cry,* and the superb *Jubilate Deo.*

Its serenity by nearly all the chaconnes or passacaglias, among which we would especially single out " Wondrous Machine " (the reference is to the organ), in the ode to Saint Cecilia for 1692; " Now the night is chased away," in *The Fairy Queen;* " Here the deities approve " (this last, which is in the first ode to Saint Cecilia, dated 1683, is a version in four-part harmony of the *New Ground* (P. S. Ed., VI, 30) from the collection of harpsichord pieces).

Its meditative repose by the Largo (third movement) of the Sixth Sonata in the collection of twelve sonatas.

Its calm and authoritative gravity by the bass solo of the Almighty: " Thou art My Son " (Psalm ii. 7), from the anthem *Why do the heathen?* (P. S. Ed., XVII, 12).

Its majestic and gentle composure by Neptune's song, in *The Tempest,* " Æolus, you must appear," which is in C minor, the air being taken up a little later in C major to the words " See, see, the Heavens smile."

Its imposing dignity by most of the symphonies that form the opening of the odes and the dramatic works.

Its solemnity, tinged with mourning, by the fragment that forms the prelude to the trio " Prepare," in *The Libertine* — only nineteen bars, alas, but how much is contained in those nineteen bars (P. S. Ed., XX, 55)!

Its despondent melancholy by the anthem " O God, Thou hast cast us out " (Psalm lx. 1, 2, 11, 12).

What depths of melancholy, again, in the

musical rendering of the Psalmist's words: "*Qui percussisti omnes inimicos meos, maxillam, dentes improborum confregisti*," from Psalm iii, *Jehovah, quam multi sunt hostes!*

What pathetic accents in the second scene of *Don Quixote* (P. S. Ed., XVI, 186) where Altisidora, the luckless maiden, sighs out her lament, only to be cut short by a dainty dance air in four-time!

What pathos again in the conclusion of the Toccata in A major (P. S. Ed., VI, 42)! But the work in which Purcell is most moving is the opera *Dido and Æneas,* above all in the well-known scene where the Queen of Carthage, forsaken by the Trojan leader, proclaims her grief and announces her approaching death to her confidante. The recitative, and the air on a ground bass in the rhythm of a passacaglia, which follows it, are poignant in their melancholy. "Art in England," says M. Romain Rolland in his biography of Handel, "has produced nothing more worthy to rank with the masterpieces of Italian art." "Let us study the last air of Dido," writes M. Paul Landormy, in his *Histoire de la musique*. "It is a fine page, which will stand comparison with any masterpiece whatsoever of the great composers."

With what scrupulous care does Purcell adapt his music to the literary text! How happily he succeeds in giving each phrase, and even each word, its maximum effect!

We do not propose to discuss the relation between the spirit of the words and the general movement of the musical phrase. This is a matter of course in all composers. It is quite obvious that one would not conceive of an Alleluia as a slow movement, or of a psalm such as *O God, Thou hast cast us out* as a rapid one. The point with which we are concerned is what we may perhaps call " verbal correspondence " — that is to say, the relation between the music and the meaning of one or several words. This was not a new idea in Purcell's day, as MM. André Pirro and Henri Quittard have pointed out in their critical essays on Heinrich Schütz and Giacomo Carissimi, published by the Schola Cantorum of Paris under the title of *Concerts spirituels*. Does not Carissimi write a trill for the bass on the word " *tremor* " in the passage from the great trio " *Undique invadit nos horror, undique tremor occupat*," in his *Lament of the Damned* (*Plainte des Damnés*) ? When, in his motet for five voices *Velociter*, Orlando de Lassus had to set the words " *descendentibus in lacum* (descending into the lake)," he used a descending figure for his voices, ending on a deep chord. Viadana, in his motet *Exultate, justi,* for four voices, had already tried to imitate in the vocal parts the plucking of the strings in the passage " *In psalterio decem chordarum psallite illi* (Play unto Him on a harp of ten strings)." There are hundreds of examples of this type. All the English musicians of the Renaissance and the Restoration conformed to this practice. It is an application of a principle sound in itself, but which, as often applied, may savour of artificiality.

There is, then, nothing surprising in the disposition of the opening bass solo in the anthem *They that go down to the sea in ships,* dedicated to the Rev. J. Gostling, which starts on the D above the staff and, covering two octaves, descends to the D below it. Such a proceeding is within the scope of any musician. The same device is found applied in the inverse sense in Dumont's *Credo,* on the words " *Et ascendit in cœlum* (He ascended into heaven)."

But where, in the five-part chorus " Come follow me," from *King Arthur,* or in Belinda's air " Pursue thy Conquest, Love," from *Dido and Æneas,* or in the charming " Swifter, Isis, swifter flow," from the ode dated 1681, Purcell has recourse to regular canon form in which the parts enter more or less close upon one another in order to emphasize the sense of the words "follow," "pursue," or "flow," he is adopting a much more ingenious device.

Elsewhere he interprets the spirit of a verse of a psalm by the writing of the vocal parts. When in the heart-broken anthem *O God, Thou hast cast us out* the words implore God's assistance, the still hesitating trust of man is represented by a slight quickening of the time; the interweaving of the choral parts becomes less close, and the division of the choir into two parts brings a ray of light into the previously sombre atmosphere of the anthem.

A still better proof of Purcell's ingenuity, in our opinion, is his handling of what we may perhaps call "harmonic correspondence." In the ode of 1689 dedicated to Queen Mary (P. S. Ed., XI, 19) he has to set the words "so great" and "so good a queen" — "great" and "good" occurring in the same bar. The word "great" is emphasized by a chord of the major sixth, immediately after which the musical phrase takes on a note of tenderness on the words "so good a queen," when Purcell uses the minor key. Notice the B flat which occurs on "good."

Our object in mentioning this is to show the care that Purcell brought to the understanding and musical interpretation of the text.

The deep sadness of the passage already quoted, " *Qui percussisti omnes inimicos meos,*" and the tragic character of Dido's great air, are both rendered by a chromatic descending figure for the bass. It is true that other masters had made use of this means of expression before Purcell. We must instance the apt use of it made by Carissimi in the air from *Ezéchias* on the words " *Et in dimidio annorum meorum vadam ad portas inferi* (And in the midst of my days I shall go down to the gates of hell)*.*" Buxtehude makes a telling use of it in his Chaconne in E minor, and later on, Bach uses it in the *Crucifixus* in his B-minor mass. The merit of the composer lies not so much in the use of a particular means of expression as in the aptness of its use, and the beauty of the effect obtained. On the other hand, what a mag-

A Shake is mark'd thus ▤ explain'd thus ▥ a beat mark'd thus ▤ explain'd thus ▥ a plain note & Shake thus ▤ explain'd thus ▥ a fore fall mark'd thus ▤ explain'd thus ▥ a back fall mark'd thus ▤ explain'd thus ▥ a mark for the turn thus ▤ explain'd thus ▥ the mark for y Shake turn'd thus ▤ explain'd thus ▥ observe that you allway's Shake from the note above and beat from y note or half note below, according to the key you play in, and for y plain note and shake if it be a note without a point you are to hold half the quantity of it plain, and that upon y note above that which is mark'd and Shake the other half, but if it be a note with a point to it you are to hold all the note plain and Shake only the point, a Star is mark'd thus ▤ explain'd thus ▥ the mark for y battery thus ▤ explain'd thus ▥ the bass Clift mark'd thus ▤ the Tenner Clift thus ▤ the Treble Clift thus ▤ a barr is mark'd thus ▤ at y end of every time that it may be the more easy to keep time, a Double bar is mark'd thus ▥ and set down at y end of every Strain, which imports you must play y Strain twice, a repeat is mark'd thus ▥ and Signifies you must repeat from y note to y end of the Strain or lesson, to know what key a tune is in, observe y last note or Close of y tune for by that note y key is nam'd, all Round O end with y first Strain.

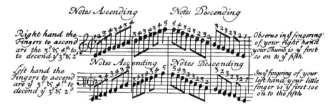

Notes Ascending   Notes Descending

Right hand the Fingers to ascend are the 3.d & 4.th to decend y 3.d & 2.d

Observe in y fingering of your right hand your Thumb is y first so on to y fifth

Notes Ascending   Notes Descending

Left hand the Fingers to ascend are y 3.d & 4.th to decend y 3.d & 2.d

In y fingering of your left hand your little finger is y first soe on to the fifth

FACSIMILE OF A PAGE FROM
PURCELL'S *Lessons*

nificent progression accompanies the words
" *Gloria mea et extollens caput meum,*" from the
anthem *Jehovah, quam multi sunt hostes!*

Purcell, like Bach after him, has recourse to
two media to interpret his musical ideas: namely,
accompanied melody and choral writing. In his
work the monodic and polyphonic styles are rec-
onciled. In speaking of John Blow we mentioned a didactic work that bears the name of
Purcell, *An Introduction to the Skill of Musick.*
This work was published by John Playford in
1655, and twelve editions appeared between
1655 and 1694. In spite of his overwhelming
labours, Purcell found time to recast the twelfth
edition and to include in it some reflections of
the greatest interest on fugue, double fugue,
fugue by augmentation, and fugue *recte et retro.*
The opening pages of this twelfth edition contain a statement, followed by precepts, concerning the accompaniment of melody. " Formerly," says Purcell, " [musicians] used to
compose from the Bass; but modern authors compose to the Soprano, when they make Counterpoint or Basses to tunes or songs." Despite our respect for Purcell's memory, we must point out
that the old musicians did not always work from
the bass. The parts were built up one above the

other, as we said above, but the bass was not invariably the starting-point in polyphonic composition. With this reservation, we agree that the characteristics of ancient music are indicated in the spirit if not in the letter of Purcell's statement. Farther on, Purcell advises the composer to reinforce the soprano part by a bass as " airy " — that is to say, as supple and *cantabile* — as the soprano part will allow. Such a recommendation is just what we should expect of Purcell, for he himself put in practice what he suggested to others. Indeed, he sometimes used a whole air as a bass; for instance, the " Quickstep " to which *Lilliburlero* was set for the jig in *The Gordian Knot Untyed*, or, as our readers will remember, the ballad " Cold and Raw " for a song in the ode of 1692 dedicated to Queen Mary.

Choral writing played an important part in Purcell's work. Many of his choruses are in five, six, seven, and eight parts, written according to the principles of the polyphonic school. He had studied the old masters, who were not content with the four voices that had become the accepted rule. Did not Tallis use forty-eight voices before he was satisfied? His motet *Spem in alium non habui* is for eight five-part choruses. Purcell

is a master of choral writing, owing to his ingenious entries for the voices and his art in making all the parts melodious. He seeks after novel
effects and succeeds in achieving them. Compare the end of his first ode to Saint Cecilia
(1683): at the words " *Io Cecilia* " the four
voices of the choir sing together; then the soprano and alto are silenced to give place to the
bass and tenor; the tenor ceases in its turn, and
the bass alone is left to finish the ode. This is a
most poetical example of a gradual decrease of
tone. In *Dido and Æneas* the voices in the
Witches' Chorus " In our deep vaulted cell "
(P. S. Ed., III, 44) are divided into two groups,
of which one echoes the other. Perhaps the idea
of this happy device was suggested to Purcell by
the technique of the organ, on which it is usual
to change the degree of sonority by passing from
one manual to another.

Purcell manages to graduate his effects by
the aid of the voices alone. The final scene of
Dioclesian, constructed entirely on a chaconne
rhythm, is full of grandeur; but the periodical
and persistent reiteration of the same motif
might in the long run produce an impression of
monotony on the listener. This is where the different voices play such a helpful role. The motif

of the passacaglia is established by the bass; then the bass, alto, and tenor unite in a trio; an orchestral interlude follows; then a repetition of the trio. This harmonious whole is crowned by a song for four voices. By the application of such devices Purcell obtains variety in unity. A similar remark may be made with regard to the fourth act of *King Arthur*.

As we remarked above, Coperario, Deering, Dowland, and Tomkins treated the viols in exactly the same fashion as voices were treated in their day. Purcell, like Handel and Bach after him, and H. Schütz, and sometimes Carissimi, before him, demanded that the voice should execute runs similar to those written for stringed instruments. The passage " Who can express the noble acts of the Lord? " in the anthem *Oh give thanks,* and the opening of the anthem *O all ye people, clap your hands* are hardly different, to the eye, from the trio *Wann unsre Augen schlafen ein* by H. Schütz or the passage " *Eamus, eamus, surgamus* " (note the triple canon) in the trio from Carissimi's *Disciples at Emmaus (Pèlerins d'Emmaüs)*. But it is necessary to distinguish between these runs and the roulades of the Italian style. The latter are excrescences upon the melodic line, which break its normal development.

The runs in Purcell, as in his forerunners and successors, are not adventitious ornaments; they are an integral part of the general economy of the piece. They enter into its contrapuntal texture and do not detach themselves from it in vocal fireworks.

When we glance at the score of certain of Purcell's compositions, we perceive, not without some dissatisfaction, that the altos descend to E and even to D below the staff; for instance, in the twelfth bar of the psalm O *God, Thou hast cast us out*. At such times we feel tempted to protest against the scant consideration that he shows for the voices. It is as well to point out that at the Restoration period the alto part was taken by a male alto, in default of women's or children's voices.

Augmentation (the increasing of the value of the notes in a fugal subject) is an eloquent means of expression, which Purcell is fond of using. We find applications of this device in the chorus " Bright Cecilia," in the 1692 ode to Saint Cecilia, after the fugal episode given to string quartet and oboes, as well as in the first Adagio of the Seventh Sonata in the collection of twelve sonatas. The Sixth Sonata opens with a double canon with augmentation at the fifth and the octave above. In fact, there is no end to the proofs that we could cite of the ingenuity and technical ability of our subject.

Another aspect of Purcell's originality is to be found in certain characteristics of his musical writing that throw his personality into sharp relief.

And here we feel bound to crave our readers' resigned indulgence for the examination of Purcell's work that occupies the next few pages. A critical analysis of Purcell's writings leads us into considerations of a technical order, which are indispensable, but a little dry.

From all time new composers have been attacked on account of their " discords." No one has been spared. Lecerf de la Viéville, Lully's biographer, writes as follows on the subject of Buononcini: " His discords are positively alarming! Harshness could go no further! . . . It is simply unbearable. Happy are those who are hard of hearing! "

Lully also had had a reputation for discords. Perrault and Titon du Tillet praised him for it. " Out of discords," they say, " he has made his finest passages." But they quickly add that " he had the art of preparing, placing, and resolving them."

How free from discords do Lully and Buononcini sound beside Purcell, who writes with a daring that would have scared these two masters. He does not always trouble to " prepare " his discords. He has a great affection for the close interval of the second. His works are crowded with examples of it. Here is an interesting example taken from the fourth ode to King Charles II (P. S. Ed., XV, 109) :

In Purcell's music we often meet with combinations of notes that at first sight seem harsh, but are quite naturally resolved in the succeeding chord. We may cite a passage in the psalm *Jehovah, quam multi sunt hostes,* at the words " *Ego cubui et dormivi,*" where a 6/5 chord falls on the " *et,*" with an E flat added in the second soprano. This E flat produces a most unusual effect. In reality it is only a passing note leading to the F in the following chord, and already sounded in the preceding one. In *Dido and Æneas,* at the third bar of the repeat in the

" Ritornello " (P. S. Ed., III, 50), note the group-
ing of the notes A, C sharp, B flat, and F. It is a
chord of the sixth on the fifth degree. The minor
key supplies the leading note as the third. Purcell boldly adds the ninth as a suspension of the
octave, giving rise to dissonances, which are quite
simply resolved on the common chord.

In the same order of ideas, we may indicate
the happy progressions by intervals of a ninth
in the passacaglia that immediately precedes the
entrance of the nymph in the fourth act of
King Arthur.

The following passage from *O God, Thou
hast cast us out* will give us some idea of the com-
plexity of Purcell's polyphonic writing and the
use he makes of suspensions and anticipations:

There is one category of discords of a special character to which we would draw the reader's particular attention. We were once showing a friend who was a great music-lover the "Ground" on page 39 of the volume of the Purcell Society's edition that contains the harpsichord pieces. At the following passage (quoted below), which recurred several times, we saw

him shudder. "And yet," he exclaimed, "you

pretend that this Purcell of yours knew how to write! Any beginner would have avoided those false relations."

Now, there is no false relation in the " Ground " in question. There are simply some peculiarities in the writing, which are to be accounted for by the form of minor scale used in the seventeenth and even in the eighteenth century. The minor scale was dimorphous; that is to say, it had a double form. It had one form ascending and another descending. The following is the form of the minor scale both ascending and descending, taking as an example the scale of C minor, the key of the " Ground " that our friend had under his eyes — though not in his ear!

But the minor scale has evolved, and today it takes this form:

The reader will notice that the interval of an augmented second separates the A flat from the B natural in the modern scale. Our musical ancestors were horrified at this interval, which they considered impracticable for the voice. We need only refer to scale No. 1 to realize that what seemed an error to our friend was absolutely correct, or at least in accordance with the practice of the day.

The contrary movements in contrapuntal writing inevitably led to clashes in the progression of the parts, of which the following are examples:

In the anthem *My beloved spake* (P. S. Ed., XIII^A, 30, fourth bar) Purcell sounds a D flat in the second violin at the same time as a D natural in the first violin. This discordance arises from the coincidence of two fragments of scales, the one ascending and the other descending. The same phenomenon is strikingly illustrated at the bottom of the same page, in the second bar, just before the cadence in F major.

In the Sixth Sonata of the collection of ten sonatas, at the first bar of page 63, we find an F natural in the bass and an F sharp in the first violin. The F sharp is a grace note below G. It seems unnecessary to multiply examples. Those we give will suffice to illustrate the theory and application of the minor scale in its double form. But we cannot insist too much on the point that there is nothing reprehensible in the application of this theory in Purcell. The dimorphous scale took form at the beginning of the sixteenth century. It may be regarded as a development of the first Gregorian mode. When we are faced with what many people have taken or take for mistakes in Purcell's composition, we must always ask ourselves if we have not before us some peculiarity of the dimorphous scale. In the immense output of this musician there are only a few points that cannot be explained, or are difficult of explanation. The chapter dealing with discords in Purcell and the sixteenth-century composers in *Music in England*, by Ernest Walker, is interesting reading.

The seventeenth-century composers used only two flats in the key signature to indicate C minor, and not three, as today, because when the voices were ascending, the A was always natural; when they descended, the A was marked with a flat throughout the piece. The bass air in Lully's *Persée*, to which we have already referred, is in G minor, but there is only one flat in the key signature.

But though there are certain passages based upon the use of the minor scale as it was known in former days that are disconcerting to our habits of ear, there are others to which it lends a very special charm. Thus, in the duet for two sopranos in the first ode to King Charles II (P. S. Ed., XV, 15) the E natural, occurring in the middle of the key of G minor, lends warmth and lightness to the melody. Indeed, the music is in complete harmony with the words:

> When the summer, in his glory,
> Was delightful, warm and gay....

The same remark as we have made on the subject of Purcell's melody applies to the first phrase sung by Mârouf in Monsieur Rabaud's work of that name. Certainly the atmosphere of the latter work is quite different from that of the English musician; in Purcell the question of exoticism could not arise. The presence of an E natural appearing in a chord of G minor suffices to produce the effect sought by the author of *Mârouf*. Thus is confirmed the power, as Boileau might have said, of a mere note, but a note in the right place.

There is another peculiarity in Purcell's writing that surprises the ear of the modern listener; namely, the frequent recourse which he has to the subdominant.

Symphonie

This fragment is the first bar of the anthem *My heart is inditing.* " Why that B flat? " we may ask; one would expect a B natural, since the piece is in C major. Very likely; but B natural with the F in the bass would make the interval of an augmented fourth, which had at all costs to be avoided. The augmented fourth, that *diabolus in musica,* was still odious to the ears of the seventeenth-century composers. It is the dread of the augmented fourth that gives us a C natural where we expect a C sharp before the final cadence in D of the Maestoso in the Second Overture to *King Arthur.* This dread was shared by all the musicians of the seventeenth century. In an air in the major key from Lully's *Le Sicilien,* " *Pauvres amants, quelle erreur d'adorer des inhumaines!* " there is a descending interval on the word " *adorer* " that to our ears would require the augmented fourth (F sharp). Lully avoids it by making the F natural.

We will not go so far as to assert that no exception is to be taken to the English master's works so far as the writing is concerned. From time to time there are curious passages that are difficult to justify, as in the ninth bar of the second repeat in the symphony which opens the fifth act of *King Arthur*. In the chaconne, or *Curtain Tune on a ground*, from the masque in *Timon of Athens* (P. S. Ed., VI, 24) the major and minor modes alternate constantly in a rather disconcerting manner. In the anthem *I will sing unto the Lord*, at the ninth and eighth bars before the end, Purcell passes from C to G major. The modulation is clumsily effected, as the dominant chord on G is sounded immediately before the cadence in G, which produces a startling false relation. In the tenor solo " The bashful Thames," from *The Yorkshire Feast Song* (P. S. Ed., I, 11, first bar), we expect a cadence on the words " and poor."

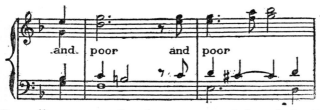

Purcell progresses by the augmented fourth in C and accentuates the faultiness of the progression by an appoggiatura on the augmented fourth. Did the composer intend to interpret the word " poor " by what might be considered a poorness in the harmony? A curious point is that, if we suppress the bar in question, the progression of the bars which precede and follow it becomes normal. Other flaws could probably be found in the master's work; they may be explained by a reason — which, after all, explains nothing — namely, the haste with which he must have written some of his compositions. But evidences of this supposed haste are so rare as to be lost in the general body of his works — *rari nantes in gurgite vasto.*

On the other hand, how sweet to the ear are the many effects that he produces by the simplest means, by the judicious use of the Neapolitan sixth (the flattened sixth in the chord of the sixth on the fourth degree of the scale) ; or by a succession of chords of the sixth — for example, in the 1681 ode to the King, at the words " Tender lovers " — or by a frequent use of the minor mode!

We ought not, of course, to exaggerate the moving properties of the minor mode. Many pieces full of melancholy and emotion are in the major key, and many merry songs are in the minor: in the Roman liturgy the anthem O *Filii et Filiæ,* for Easter Sunday, and the *Veni, Sancte Spiritus,* sung on Whit Sunday, are in the minor; the *Stabat mater dolorosa* is in the major. However, the properties that are generally ascribed to each of these modes must have some relation with reality for Molière to have written, in *Le Sicilien,* evidently under the influence of Lully: " No; I want something tender and passionate, something that lulls me in a gentle reverie." Such are the words of Adraste; to which Hali replies: " I see plainly that you are in favour of the *bémol.* But there is a way of satisfying us both: they will have to sing you a scene from a little comedy that I saw them rehearsing. Two shepherds, languishing with love, appear one after the other in a wood and utter their laments in the *bémol,* after which they relate to each other the cruelty of their mistresses; upon which in comes a merry shepherd with a fine melody in the *bécarre,* who makes fun of their weakness."

In this passage " *bémol* " signifies the minor mode, and " *bécarre* " the major.

Purcell also displays great variety in his cadences. It sometimes happens that he employs the perfect cadence in the style of Lully: on a

dominant root, having normally sounded the octave to the bass with a fifth superimposed, before
resolving on the tonic chord he makes the octave
and fifth each fall one tone, making two con-
secutive fifths; that is to say, the octave, before
its resolution, passes through the seventh of the
dominant, while the fifth anticipates the tonic,
which will be heard in the next chord.

We may next point out the final cadence in
the 1681 ode to Charles II (P. S. Ed., XV, 51).
The descending alto part produces a charmingly
melodious effect. For great occasions Purcell
makes use of the plagal cadence, with its markedly dignified character. It is with this cadence that he terminates the solemn anthem
Thou knowest, Lord, the secret of our hearts,
and his *Te Deum* and *Jubilate,* on the word
" Amen." The plagal sometimes appears with a
variant.

The cadence with the most characteristic
savour to be found in Purcell's work — and it is a
truly English one — is that which consists in the
employment of a chord of the sixth on the dominant, resolving on the common chord. Sometimes this chord of the sixth is embellished by the
seventh. This is the form in which it appears in
Chopin's Second Ballade.

Cadence No. 1 occurs in the chorus " We have sacrificed," from *King Arthur,* at the words " Our defender "; cadence No. 2, in the Harvest Home chorus in the fifth act of the same work.

The ear familiar with pluritonality will find little complication in Purcell's harmonic system. If, however, we examine his compositions, not only in the light of historical criticism, but in themselves, we are led to the conclusion that his writing is daring, and much more daring than that of his contemporaries.

Purcell is also in advance of his time in the art of modulation. Certainly there are times when he does not venture outside the more nearly related keys. To us, who are growing more and more accustomed to passing through a succession of keys, certain of his compositions err by an abuse of perfect cadences in the original key; for instance, in the anthems *Thy word is a lantern* (Psalm cxix. 105), *Be merciful unto me*

(Psalm lvi. 1), *My beloved spake* (Song of Songs, ii. 10). In this last anthem, however, the intervention of the key of F minor introduces an element of variety. . . . With a few reservations, we may say that when it suits Purcell's fancy to modulate, he indulges in it to his heart's content. He seems to take a pleasure in displaying the colours of his harmonic palette, as, for instance, in the " *Sicut erat* " of his anthem *Beati omnes qui timent Dominum*. This fragment begins in E flat; soon we are in A major, a key far removed from that of the opening; we next come to a section in E major; after which Purcell skilfully leads us to a final cadence in C minor (the key of the anthem itself), passing through the keys of C, F, and G minor. The passage " *Qui percussisti*," from the anthem *Jehovah, quam multi sunt hostes*, opens on a chord of F major and concludes in the key of G. The third movement (Presto) of the First Sonata in the collection of twelve sonatas may be cited as an example of tonal variety.

In the field of modulation Purcell sometimes has surprises in store for his hearers. In the Frost Scene from *King Arthur*, at the words " Whose kind and constant hearts will Love embrace " we might expect a cadence in A minor:

the music preceding the D minor chord on the word " kind " seems to announce it. Purcell, however, leaves us in the key of D minor. In Air No. 4 from *Bonduca* (P. S. Ed., XVI, 52), at the third bar, we have the feeling that Purcell is leading us to the key of B flat by the 6/4 chord. Not at all: he resolves this 6/4 chord on the chord of the seventh, on the second degree of the E-flat scale, and returns through the ninth to the dominant of C minor, the original key of the piece.

The examples that we have given of Purcell's style of writing will, we hope, suffice to show how skilful he was in avoiding the commonplace.

And now, after this somewhat dry analysis, let us proceed to synthesis. We have not drawn any distinction between the secular and the religious music of Purcell. This is because his modes of expression and workmanship are really the same in both. Both have a common source of inspiration — his dramatic sense.

It would be absurd to conclude from the introduction of secular forms into ecclesiastical art, as it was conceived by Purcell, that his sacred works are animated by a spirit which the Church could not admit or tolerate. There are in existence two documents that reveal a truly religious turn of mind in Purcell, at least at certain periods of his life. One is a page in the collection of manuscripts preserved in the Fitzwilliam Museum at Cambridge, and the other is his will. On the page in question we read these words, in the composer's own handwriting: " God bless Mr. Henry Purcell. September the 10th 1682." The will opens with the words: " In the name of God. Amen."

The fact that Purcell was much attached to the Church of England is proved by a document which, beneath its frivolous appearance, enlightens us as to the nature of his religious tendencies. It is a drinking-song, a catch for three voices, published in 1701 in the second book of the *Pleasant Musical Companion,* and reproduced in the twenty-second volume of the Purcell Society's edition.

True Englishmen drink a good health to the Mitre;
Let our Church ever flourish, tho' her enemies spite
    her;
May their cunning and forces no longer prevail,
But their malice as well as their arguments fail!
Then remember the Seven who supported our cause,
As stout as our martyrs, and as just as our laws.

The " Seven " here referred to are the seven bishops who protested against the second Declaration of Indulgence issued by James II, on April 27, 1688, and were consequently imprisoned in the Tower of London.

Purcell could not but be glad when, under the influence of Charles II, the rites and ceremonies of the Church of England were restored, for, by adding dignity to the forms of worship and increasing the pomp of religious services, this was favourable to the production of musical works on a larger scale and of a more solemn character. The impressions that Purcell received in his tenderest youth in the dark, mysterious shades of Westminster Abbey, where a dim light filters through the transept windows; the emotions which he experienced amid the hushed meditation of the crowd, in an atmosphere where the memories of ancient times mingled with the vision of those dear to him; the grave organ tones, and the harmonious sweetness of the choir, which he had heard as a boy, echoing beneath the vaulted Gothic roof; all these influences must surely have produced a powerful effect upon his sensitive nature, and contributed more than any theological arguments could have done towards increasing his attachment to a doctrine that the venerable Abbey church had come to symbolize in his eyes. And, indeed, nobody in the least familiar with musical history can mention Purcell, or hear him mentioned, without being conscious, as it were, of the vast mass of Westminster Abbey looming in the background. Or who can tread these hallowed stones, beneath which so many of the glorious dead sleep their last, without evoking the shade of the famous artist, which floats, and will for ever float, among the columns and beneath the arches of the august collegiate church, whose religious ceremonies owe so much of their magnificence to the nobility of his genius?

But whatever the exact nature of his religious beliefs may have been, his church music is not mystical in character. It does not produce the contemplative mood from which springs ecstasy; it leaves us upon earth. Purcell is, however, guided by the words of the Bible, the very essence of which is revealed to him by the instinctive promptings of his intelligence and sensibility. His music reflects the spirit of his text, whether this be austere, despondent to the point of despair, or full of gaiety and pastoral charm. Our souls are stirred by changing emotions as we yield ourselves to Purcell's musical interpretation of the Psalmist's verses. Under his hands they assume what may almost be called a scenic character. Solos alternate with vocal ensembles and instrumental episodes in such a way as to lend an essentially dramatic character to his religious compositions. We hasten to add that, though they are dramatic in character, they are in no sense theatrical. Purcell never aims at mere effectiveness by means of an artificial and histrionic eloquence, which does not ring true.

King Charles II was no stranger to the dramatic conception of sacred music. The " Merry Monarch " could not follow the complexities of the polyphonic style. The problems of counterpoint left him cold. His frivolous nature was intolerant of those pieces in which the composer developed his four, five, six, seven, or eight parts without flagging from the beginning to the final close. The King loved variety.

The monodic style had become a great menace to the existence of polyphony. Charles II encouraged its development as much as he was able. When still quite young (he was seventeen years old), he had heard Luigi Rossi's opera *Orfeo* at the French court in 1647, and he had never forgotten it. His desire was that church music should be modelled upon secular music, and that to a very marked degree. Charles further liked all music, even sacred music, to be very rhythmic. Pepys tells us that he enjoyed beating time to it with a movement of his hand or foot.

Musicians of riper years were not successful in the type of music that enjoyed royal favour. Such men as Lowe, Christopher Gibbons, and Childe remained faithful to the polyphonic style, in which William Byrd and Orlando Gibbons had shone. Captain Cooke and, following his leading, his pupils fell in with the King's views, at least to a certain extent. They had recourse to all the devices of dramatic expression that might charm the ear and move the heart. Most fortunately, led by their good taste and sense of artistic fitness, and thanks to the employment of a contrapuntal style, whether imitative or fugal, they were able to combine the dignity demanded by the ecclesiastical manner with the resources of the lyrical style.

In fact, though the King succeeded in imposing his preference for forms comparatively novel on England, to which composers had now to adapt their musical inspiration, the latter, for their part, interpreted his wishes or desires in their own way, and imposed their conception of the art of composition on him. Charles II once asked John Blow to write a piece in the style of Carissimi's *Dite, O cieli* (which that artist did by composing the cantata *Go, perjured man*) ; but it must not be concluded that he hampered the freedom of the composers in the rendering of their conceptions. It is simply a proof of his taste for the music of the Italian master.

We must place it to Purcell's credit that he eliminated from his religious compositions the fantastic embellishments which Carissimi had made fashionable. Sir Hubert Parry, in his volume of the *Oxford History of Music,* speaks of the latter as a great sinner in this respect. " If we compare any recitative of Lully's with one of Carissimi's," says Monsieur L. de la Laurencie, " we see that the director of music to the Grand Monarque has, so to speak, applied a cleansing process to Italian technique: he has weeded out of the garden of monody all those rank growths which the vogue for *bel canto* had allowed to flourish, and which were, indeed, inherent in the music of the day." Purcell did well to follow Lully's example. Except in his organ pieces and the pieces for the harpsichord published in the same volume of the Purcell Society's edition — for of course organ technique and that of the clavecin or harpsichord were taught according to much the same rules — we find hardly any embellishments.

There is a family likeness between the music of all Captain Cooke's pupils, due to the adoption of similar forms; yet each has his own separate personality. We can easily see that the works of William Turner, Sampson Estwick, Thomas Tudway, and Henry Hall — at least those that we have had the opportunity of seeing — are of a markedly scholastic character. They are in an elevated, but very often stiffly formal style. Michael Wise surpasses them in the elegance and charm of his melodic vein. His quick temper was but one side of a sensitive nature, to which his works bear witness.

John Blow occupies a great place in the history of English music. He left a large number of works of every sort: songs, harpsichord or organ pieces, a sonata for organ and violin, odes in honour of Saint Cecilia or for New Year's Day, and some hundred anthems. Throughout his whole life he wavered between the monodic and polyphonic styles, but leaves us definitely under the impression that he was more at his ease in the latter. His best works, in our opinion, are the odes *Great Janus; Great Sir, the Joy of all Hearts; and The Birth of Love* — in which vocal ensembles in five or six parts predominate — and the anthems *God is our Hope and Strength; O God, Wherefore art Thou absent?* and *My God, look upon me* — in which the voices are so intricately interwoven as to produce a rich and finely knit body of sound. *God is our Hope and Strength* is a chorus for eight voices; *O God, Wherefore art Thou absent?* is for five; in this last chorus grief is at once simply and eloquently expressed by the interval of a diminished fourth. John Blow was a musical writer of consummate skill. Side by side with these specimens of the polyphonic style we may enjoy certain melodies of his that have an almost Purcellian freshness. The work of John Blow as a whole is full of nobility, but of a nobility that is somewhat frigid. It is to be regretted that even his muse, so often austere in mood, often succumbed to a weakness for Italian embellishments.

With the exception of Henry Purcell, Pelham Humphrey was the most naturally gifted musician of his time; indeed it was only because his exceptional gifts had impressed those who came in contact with him that he was sent to Paris. Under the guidance of Lully he was bound to develop his sense of rhythm, while at the same time new modes of expression were revealed to him. What is entirely his own is the pathos with which his works are instinct, particularly in the anthems *Haste Thee, O God, to deliver me; Thou art my King; Hear, O Heavens; Like as the hart,* published by Dr. Boyce (1710–79) a hundred years later in his three-volume collection of *Cathedral Music; Have Mercy upon me, O God,* mentioned by Pepys in his *Diary,* the spirited *Rejoice in the Lord,* and *O God, my God, why hast Thou forsaken me?* in which we would draw particular attention to the moving bass solo with which it opens. There are strains of Pelham Humphrey's which might have raised hopes of the dawn of a fine musical genius; these hopes came to fruition in Purcell, who was for a time his pupil, and in whom the predominant qualities of each of the composers named above were combined in a heightened degree with his own.

While Purcell gave a dramatic turn to his religious works, in his secular compositions, on the other hand — odes, sonatas, suites, comedies, and tragedies — he drew largely upon the treasures of his contrapuntal science, and frequently had recourse to the imitative and fugal styles, which are looked upon — or used to be — as alone suitable to the expression of religious sentiment. We would indicate as very fine examples of the fugal style the Allegro (P. S. Ed., XXI, 63) from Gould's tragedy *The Rival Sisters,* the second part of the overture to the third Welcome Song (P. S. Ed., XV, 53), the chorus *Fill every heart with love of thee,* from the ode to Saint Cecilia of 1692 (P. S. Ed., VIII, 13). In a letter to the famous actor David Garrick, dated September 3, 1775, Dr. Arne wrote that Purcell's dramatic music, though excellent in itself, was cathedral music, in no way adapted to a modern theatrical audience. But did the forms adopted by Purcell, and later on by Bach and Handel, ever hamper the soaring flight of their inspiration?

Few musicians have possessed the melodic sense to such a degree as Purcell; and this is one of the reasons to which we must ascribe the impression of unity produced in us by his work as a whole. Not the slightest trace of effort can be felt in the melodies of the English master, they spring spontaneously to life. Purcell sings as naturally as a bird. There is hardly one of his compositions in which the singing quality flags; sometimes it is thrown into relief by a rich harmonic background, sometimes by a closely knit contrapuntal tissue; sometimes it is blended with one or the other; but from beginning to end of the piece the song pours forth with an ease and plenitude comparable to those of Mozart, Schubert, or Fauré, broken only by an occasional comma. Melody flows through all Purcell's works like blood in the body, both in his vocal ensembles and in his symphonies. His quest for contrapuntal combinations of the most complicated kind does not absorb his attention to such a point as to paralyse his melodic faculties. Even in the solution of the most arduous musical problems — double canons in contrary motion, canons *recte et retro,* etc. — the feeling for melody never deserts him; which proves that technique has never been the death of inspiration, as so many people believe or affect to believe — for very good reasons!

Purcell's melody has the limpidity and elegance of Lully's, with the addition of a rarer and more aristocratic distinction, which, contradictory as it may appear, is at the same time more familiar. We may compare it to a young lady who, without knowing or intending it, is accessible to everyone, and who, while never distant, remains none the less a " great lady." Springing as it does from the heart, Purcell's melody goes straight to ours, and speaks to it like an intimate friend, for it has an infinite tenderness. Tenderness is the predominant feeling in all Purcell's work, or rather the one in which all the others seem to be fused. It is so blended with them as to produce innumerable pages that are really masterpieces of deep and subtle feeling. We may quote a few at random, though it is impossible to enumerate even the finest of them exhaustively: " I attempt from Love's sickness to fly in vain," " They tell us that your mighty power above," from *The Indian Queen,* " Fairest Isle, all isles excelling." We may also cite " The Knotting Song," a setting of Sir Charles Sedley's charming words:

> " Hears not my Phillis how the birds
>   Their feathered mates salute?
>   They tell their passion in their words,
>   Must I alone be mute? "
>   Phillis, without frown or smile,
>   Sat and knotted all the while.

> " So many months in silence past,
>   And yet in raging love,
>   Might well deserve one word at last
>   My passion should approve."
>   Phillis, without frown or smile,
>   Sat and knotted all the while.

"Must then your faithful swain expire
And not one look obtain,
Which he to soothe his fond desire
Might pleasingly explain?"
Phillis, without frown or smile,
Sat and knotted all the while.

Also "On the Brow of Richmond Hill," the words of which were composed, strange to say, by that extravagant and rather cynical humorist Tom d'Urfey, so different from Honoré d'Urfé, his French kinsman, as may be judged from the following verses:

On the brow of Richmond Hill,
Which Europe scarce can parallel,
Every eye such wonders fill,
To view the prospect round;
By whose fair and fruitful site
The silver Thames doth softly glide,
Meadows drest in summer's pride
With verdant beauties crown'd.

Lovely Cynthia passing by
With brighter glories blest my eye.
Ah! then in vain, in vain, said I,
The fields and flow'rs do shine.
Nature in this charming place

Created pleasure in excess,
But all is poor to Cynthia's face,
Whose features are divine.

We may add to the list of particularly capti-
vating melodies: " There's not a swain," from
John Fletcher's piece *Rule a wife and have a wife;*
observe in this melody the ingenious ascending
movement of the voice part, with its broken
line, on the words " Can you be? " We may further cite: " What shall I do? " from *Dioclesian;*
" Shall I? " in the third part of *Don Quixote;*
" Oh the sweet delights of Love! " from *Dioclesian;* and " Vouchsafe, O Lord, to keep us this
day without sin," from the *Te Deum* and
Jubilate.

" Purcell's music," says M. Paul Landormy,
in his *Histoire de la musique,* " is not that of a
subtly intellectual nature, but rather of a sensitive and passionate one." Indeed almost all his
songs have love for their theme, and usually un-
happy love. He enters into the finest shades of
tender sensibility. Both his melodic line and his
harmonization have inflexions that produce in us
a feeling of pain — but it is an exquisite pain.
Purcell's tenderness creates an atmosphere in
which one's soul finds comfort; it may wound,

but it always stirs our emotion and warms our heart.

Purcell has none of the " imperial calm " that, according to M. Romain Rolland, characterizes the work of Carissimi. The author of *L'Opéra en Europe avant Lully et Scarlatti* says in another passage that, " like Palestrina, Raphael, and the great school of Roman artists in general, Carissimi has the splendid gift of impersonality. . . . He has a power of endowing the tragic emotions with which his soul is filled with that serene, impersonal form which makes his sorrows, as it were, the very voice of Pain." Nothing could be less impersonal than the art of the English master. Two acute critics, MM. A. Lambinet and E. Fannière, once summed him up to us in the words: " He is the Alfred de Musset of music." Though living at a period when English writers were feeling the influence of classic art and of the great writers of France — Boileau in particular — Purcell is a romantic; and this at an epoch when reason held the exuberance of imagination and sensibility in check, and Dryden's sway was preparing for that of Pope, and heralding the literary dictatorship of Dr. Samuel Johnson. " A just and natural style of declamation, which, none the less, carefully avoids all

excess in expression and is capable of transforming a commonplace libretto into a cry of passion "
— such is the character of Carissimi's declama-
tory passages, according to M. Romain Rolland,
the author of *Musiciens d'autrefois*. Purcell, too,
draws effects of an infinite pathos from the poor-
est verses. What could be feebler than the poetry
of Nahum Tate, and, above all, the libretto of
Dido and Æneas?

The tender quality of Purcell's work is free
from all admixture of languor or of lifeless
preciosity. His nature may have had a feminine
side, but it was in no way effeminate. It was certainly no effeminate being who could write those
Canzone whose strains, by their mingled sweetness and vigour, recall the verse of Racine.

Though Purcell is an honour to European
art, he is nevertheless essentially English. He is
English in the resolute march of his melodic line,
which reminds one of the bearing of a young
Englishwoman. He is English in his cadences, in
the touch of sternness that is sometimes to be felt
in his writing. In the biographical notice which
forms the preface to his edition of Henry Purcell's harpsichord pieces, Farrenc wrote that
" Purcell's pieces, as compared with those of
Chambonnières, François Couperin, and other

clavecin writers of the same epoch, are remarkable for a certain originality, which cannot escape a practised ear." We may remark that the pieces of Chambonnières and Couperin have also their own originality, which seems to have escaped Farrenc's notice.

In what, then, does this originality consist, which Farrenc fails to define, but which does indeed distinguish not only the clavecin pieces, but also, and in a still higher degree, others of Purcell's compositions? M. Julien Tiersot supplies the answer in the *Revue de musicologie* for February 1925 (p. 39), where he says: " We find in Purcell's songs an indefinable quality redolent of the soil and wearing, as it were, a national physiognomy." Purcell does, indeed, often find his inspiration in popular tunes, and frequently indulges in the lilting rhythms dear to the English. In the prelude to his anthem *Rejoice in the Lord alway* (Philippians, iv. 4), known as the Bell Anthem, he introduces a descending scale, as of the bells that call the faithful to divine service. This Sunday memory of pealing bells is grateful to an English ear, recalling, as it does, impressions which are all the sweeter for being closely associated with those of earliest childhood. " Church bells," says M. Georges Dubosc, in the

Journal de Rouen for November 20, 1925, " are so intimately bound up with local life that they seem to belong to our very family. . . . Even those who have no religious beliefs cannot help feeling a certain tenderness for the fair maids of bronze — as the bell-ringers of Bruges call them — whose voices, melancholy and joyous by turn, arouse in us so many memories, in spite of ourselves, and whose charm is always strongest, for those who are musicians, when their notes fall dropping through the twilight." Another characteristically English feature in Purcell is his taste for subjects connected with the sea, a taste that is particularly displayed in *The Tempest*.

In spite of the circumstances in which he was placed, in spite of the artificial atmosphere in which he lived, he never lost touch with nature. In his pastoral scenes he reduces to a minimum the conventional features that the taste of the day demanded. He brings a healthy, open-air spirit into these scenes, and in this, too, he is very English.

But the most fundamentally English quality of all in Purcell lies, in our opinion, in the fusion of varied and even contradictory sentiments in the texture of his compositions. Lully, whose work has the imposing formality of a French

garden, observes the distinction of styles prescribed by the French dramatic theorists of the
seventeenth century and after. Purcell, in true
English fashion, blends them in one and the same
work. The latter has more spontaneity and fancy,
and his work may therefore be better compared
to an English park. How often a playful, merry
passage is mitigated by a touch of tender, subtle
melancholy, even in some of his ballet music!
Sometimes this contrast of opposing emotions is
pushed to its extreme limit — for instance, in the
Frost Scene from *King Arthur*. This scene contains a solo sung by Goodman Winter, which is
taken up by the chorus. Purcell brings on to the
stage inhabitants of the northern climes, numb
and shivering with cold. A dramatic situation of
a similar order had previously been devised by
Lully and Cesti, and Colasse in turn was to treat
it, in 1695, in his ballet *Les Saisons*. While most
probably drawing his inspiration from the example set by Act IV of Lully's opera *Isis*, which
was performed for the first time at Saint-
Germain-en-Laye before Louis XIV on January
5, 1677, Purcell none the less managed to main-
tain his originality. Lully's scene is for chorus
only. The choruses of the Florentine and the English master, neither of which have any connexion

with the plot, have to interpret verses that have a certain similarity; both settings consist of a melodic series of quavers vertically harmonized. But, striking as are the resemblances between them, the differences are far more so. Lully's chorus is for three voices: male alto, tenor, and bass; it is short, containing only twelve bars, which are repeated in the second verse. Purcell's chorus is for four voices — soprano, alto, tenor, and bass — and is elaborately developed. But it is not so much the form in which the two choruses are cast, as the spirit which animates them, that makes us realize how great is the difference between the conception of the two composers. Lully's is humorous, but with an amiable serenity. Purcell's is also humorous; as M. Adolphe Julien writes, in the *Journal des Débats* for December 21, 1924: " See how amusingly Purcell imitates the trembling and chattering of teeth produced by the cold, but becoming less violent as the reviving breath of love infuses new life into all his characters " — that is to say, into Goodman Winter and the persons in his train. None the less, Purcell's humour is thrown into relief against a background of a gloomy and painfully expressive cast. In him the comic and the tragic elements are so closely bound up with each other that it is hard to know which of them is the stronger. Purcell is romantic and almost Shaksperian in the Frost Scene, one of the finest and most picturesque that ever came from his pen. While certain of his works — notably *The Fairy Queen* and *The Tempest* — have a certain aerial and unsubstantial quality, this Frost Scene is tinged with that mystery which is so dear to the northern soul. We must add that the harmonies of the Florentine master are simple and free from discordant effects, while those of Purcell are, for that period, complex and rugged. Chords of the augmented fifth are introduced from time to time to lend a spice to the text. In the ninth bar of the chorus we find two of them in succession, the second leading to an augmented fourth, which is resolved on a chord of the sixth. " We must not look for harmonic refinements in the operas of Lully," says M. Henri Prunières, " for that composer held them in small esteem." " Lully takes no interest in the details of harmonization and orchestration. Once the voice part is created, the rest is only supplementary; he writes the bass part and makes his pupils work it out." So speaks M. Landormy. Purcell does not strain after harmonic refinements; they rise naturally to his pen. For him the musical idea and the form in which he clothes it appear before his mind's eye simultaneously; he thinks in terms of melody, harmony, or counterpoint at one and the same moment.

As a whole, Purcell's Frost Scene is more imposing and richer than that of Lully, and we may say this without in the least intending to exalt the English musician to the detriment of a master whose title to glory has been established by so many writers.

Few natures have been so many-sided as that of Purcell. In the merry, jovial, fantastic turn of his mind, combined with a desire to attain the highest ideals (Tudway, who knew him well, says that his ambitions were of the noblest), and in the faculties with which he was so richly endowed, he was a true son of the English Renaissance.

The more we study the works of this great artist, the more we deplore the fact that he was prevented by a premature death from completing the full course of his development. He was for ever extending the scope of the field of music in which he worked.

The development of his genius was not marked by abrupt changes in his style. Up to the end of his life he continued to make use of the means of expression that he had adopted at the opening of his career. But his style never ceased to gain in breadth as the years went by. Purcell has been criticized— and not without some justification — for failing to realize his artistic conceptions to the full. Many of his anthems open in a masterly way, only to stop short before long; others are so cut up into brief fragments as to form, not a solid musical whole, but a series of disjointed scraps. Some of his compositions produce the impression of mere sketches, though sketches of undoubted genius. How is this fragmentary character of his musical ideas to be explained? Was Purcell attempting to satisfy Charles II's taste for variety? Possibly so, though he showed considerable artistic independence in so often adopting the polyphonic style, of which his sovereign did not think very highly. Was his genius mobile rather than robust? Very probably; but it is equally probable that he was engrossed in the effort to follow the words closely, and so found himself obliged to clip the wings of his inspiration; for verses of Psalms are often very short, and express constant changes of mood. However this may be, the day came when these wings, while losing nothing of their agility, gained in strength and enabled him to soar through vast regions. There is grandeur to be found in *Diocle-sian;* we have already used this word in con-nexion with the Chaconne which closes that dra-matic work. There is grandeur in *Dido and Æneas;* in fact, this is one of the reasons which justify us in concluding that that opera is not the work of quite a young man. There is gran-deur in the anthem *My heart is inditing,* in *The Tempest,* in the odes to St. Cecilia — especially that of the year 1692 — in *The Yorkshire Feast Song,* and, above all, in the Service in B flat, *King Arthur,* and the *Te Deum.* This grandeur is sometimes inherent in the very nature of the musical conception itself, sometimes due to a skilful gradation of tone-colour, to the length-ening of rhythmic values, or to the decorative quality of the vocal and orchestral ensembles, which already foreshadow Handel's manner.

The orchestral material at Purcell's disposal consisted of the violins, including the alto and bass violins, the flute, oboe, and bassoon, the trumpet and kettledrums — very scanty re-sources in comparison with those that go to make up our modern orchestras; but he none the less succeeded in turning them to account with rare skill. The sole function of the oboes and flutes in ensemble passages had previously been to

double the strings; Purcell emancipated them.
Thus the bass solo in the chaconne " Wondrous
machine," of the 1692 ode to St. Cecilia, is accompanied by the oboes; the tenor solo " The
bashful Thames," in *The Yorkshire Feast Song,*
is supported by two flutes. It goes without saying
that an instrumental accompaniment blends with
the flutes and oboes. Purcell frequently writes
passages in which wind and stringed instruments
are contrasted. In the duet " Hark, each tree,"
from the 1692 ode, he uses three flutes, one of
them a bass flute, in alternation with violins. He
also obtained happy and novel effects by the use
of the trumpet, which he appears to have introduced into church music in England, and by
passages in which the wind and strings answer one
another. We freely admit that, as M. Prunières
has pointed out, Lully had already sought to en-
hance the tone of the various instruments by
placing them in juxtaposition. But Purcell carried the principles of orchestration laid down by
his famous predecessor very much further. It
should be noticed that the progress of Purcell's
orchestration proceeded hand in hand with the
expansion of his creative genius. When the or-
chestra is reinforced by the organ in ensemble
passages — for instance, in those of the *Te Deum*

— we feel that the body of sound created by Purcell is completely adequate. The way has now been prepared for Handel.

Purcell, with the aid of Charles II, can claim the merit of having brought the violin into more general use in England. In any case, he did not care for the nasal tone of the viols. One day he asked a friend to write some comic verses with the object of caricaturing the viol da gamba, and composed a three-part catch on them (which is to be found in Vol. XXII of the Purcell Society's edition, p. 9). The verses are as follows:

Of all the instruments that are,
None with the viol can compare;
Mark how the strings in order keep,
With a whet, whet, whet and a sweep, sweep, sweep!
But above all, this still abounds,
With a zingle, zingle, zing and a zit-zan-zounds!

Purcell dedicated his catch to the Rev. J. Gostling, who had a decided taste for the viol da gamba — a good illustration of his sense of humour.

It may, indeed, be regretted that Purcell did not have recourse to double stopping. He was certainly not acquainted with the German Biber (1638–98), who did much to improve the technique of violin-playing by the use that he made of this method. Why did not Purcell make the violinists of his day change positions? His orchestral effects would thereby have gained in brilliancy. Yet he must have heard of Baltzar. Purcell rarely goes beyond the C by extension of the first position. He very seldom ventures beyond this limit; but we find the D of the third position, notably in the Largo of the Tenth Sonata in the collection of twelve sonatas (P. S. Ed., V, 83). Purcell's timidity in the sphere of violin technique, as compared with his bold innovations in other departments of his art, is in all probability to be explained by the fear of playing out of tune. And, as a matter of fact, Handel is scarcely bolder in his sonatas than Purcell.

It looked as though the year 1683, the date at which the first collection of sonatas was published, was to mark a turning-point in the development of the composer's genius. The reference which he makes in the preface to the " levity and balladry " of the French suggests that he cherished the intention of ceasing to write ballet music, and perhaps even incidental music for plays. Later on, the theatre was to claim him once more. The composition of the sonatas is a magnificent essay in the sphere of chamber music, which was crowned with success. There has been much discussion as to which of the Italian masters Purcell took as his guide. Of all the composers whose names have been mentioned, Giovanni Battista Vitali seems to be the one to whom the Engglish musician approaches most closely; and this is also the opinion of Mr. Fuller Maitland in his article on Purcell in the *Dictionary of National Biography*. If we compare Vitali's twelve sonatas for two violins with *basso continuo* (dedicated to the " illustrissimo signore Vincenzo-Mario Carrati " and published at Bologna in 1671 by Giacomo Monti) with Purcell's twelve sonatas, we can feel but little doubt of the artistic kinship between the two masters. But a comparative examination of their work makes it abundantly plain that, whether in variety, vigour, pathos, the charm of his inspiration, or the ingenuity of his contrapuntal writing, Purcell far outstrips his model. And what we have stated with regard to the collection of twelve sonatas applies equally well to that of ten sonatas. It was probably through the agency of Charles II that Purcell became acquainted with Vitali's work. In any case, it is certain that it was the King who suggested to Purcell the idea of composing the first set of sonatas; for in the dedication we read: " They are the immediate results of your Majesties Royall favour."

3.

Purcell's Affinity with
Handel, Bach, and Present-day Musicians

IN THE COURSE of this study we have more than once ventured to associate the names of Handel and Bach with that of Purcell. It is far from our intention to place him on an equality with these two giants. But, none the less, he very frequently gives us, as it were, a foretaste of their work. In the generous warmth of their inspiration, many of his vocal ensembles wear quite a Handelian aspect; the same is true of his symphonies, owing at times to their good-tempered spirit, at times to their gravity, and of the Largos of his sonatas, with their pathetic accents. Many of his melodies are, as it were, the elder sisters of Handel's airs, with the addition of something more intimate and delicate. Everybody knows that Handel adopted many motives which pleased him in the work of others, and made them his own. In past times the originality of the musical idea was not considered as important as it is nowadays. As Grove says, the musical idea was to the musician what a text is to the preacher. The essential thing was to present it in a novel guise. Handel cannot have failed to notice the role played by the chorus in Purcell's music. He landed in England in 1710. His first Italian opera, *Rodrigo*, composed in 1707, and his serenata *Aci, Galatea e Polifemo*, written in 1708, contain no choruses. But when, towards 1720, he returned to the subject of Acis and Galatea, he inserted two choruses in the first act and four in the second. The dotted rhythm, so beloved of Purcell, does not appear at all — or, at any rate, scarcely appears in the 1708 version of *Acis*. In that of 1720, on the other hand, it expresses the characteristic mood of the air " When shall I seek the charming fair? " and of the five-part chorus " Galatea, dry thy tears." It is strange how often we have heard listeners by no means lacking in either taste or musical experience exclaim, on hearing some work of Purcell's: " Why, that is pure Handel! " — unaware of the fact that Handel (not to speak of Bach) was only ten years old at the death of the English musician.

On the other hand, Purcell's affinity with Bach can be traced in many of his Allegros and Canzone; in his moving setting of the hundredth psalm (P. S. Ed., VI) ; in the duet " Brigantium [i.e., York], honoured with a race divine," in *The Yorkshire Feast Song*, in which the stirring trumpet tones rise above the string quartet (P. S. Ed., I, 6) ; in the frequent use that he makes of the figure ♪♪♪ ; in the close texture of his contrapuntal writing, especially in the sonatas for two violins and clavecin (or harpsichord) ; in the descending leaps of a diminished fourth or fifth in the bass; and in his endeavours after novel effects of tone-colour. The characteristic qualities of his writing prepare us for the full enjoyment of the marvellous harmonic inventions of the Eisenach master. Our own personal impression has the support of M. Paul Landormy's judgment, as expressed in his *Histoire de la musique* (p. 84). " Purcell's music," he says, " is sound music, with a strong, vital rhythm, and a tragic profundity, which is often impressive and reminds us of Bach."

The mere fact that, owing to an error, the English master's Toccata in A is included in the Bach Gesellschaft's edition of the latter's works speaks volumes. The differences of detail which appear in the Toccata in the German edition and that of the Purcell Society respectively do not affect its general character. In a solid article bearing the signature of Richard Buchmayer in the *Sammelbände der Internationalen Musikgesellschaft* (for 1900–1, II, 272) we read: " There is really no particular reason for doubting that this composition is from the pen of Purcell." And a few lines below he adds: " It is extremely possible that J. S. Bach was acquainted with this work."

The character of these three masters, Handel, Bach, and Purcell, is reflected in their portraits. Handel, portly, jovial, and robust, seems made to break down all obstacles as though in sport. In J. S. Bach, with his eye aglow with intelligence, we are conscious of a perfect balance of all the faculties, combined with an irresistible strength, which is always master of itself. In Purcell there is a touch of mischief about the corners of the mouth, but his mischief has nothing aggressive about it. His glance is at times caressing, as in the portrait in which Clostermann has painted him with a roll of music in his hand; at times ardent and full of fire, as in that in the National Portrait Gallery (see Frontispiece). His hands are beautiful, and his expression is alluded to in some verses in the second volume of the *Orpheus Britannicus:*

A conqu'ring sweetness in his Visage dwelt.
His eyes would warm; his Wit, like lightning, melt.

So far as music is concerned, the three masters belong in all essentials to the same race. The genius of Bach and Handel had time to reach the highest pitch of maturity. Their work reflects the splendour of their summer and the magnificence of their autumnal years. That of Henry Purcell, apart from certain touches which reveal an early maturity, reflects the soft charm and freshness of nature in springtime, but also the slight crudity of its tones.

But there are many points of resemblance that we might bring out between Purcell and other masters besides Bach and Handel. We may quote a phrase of the English master's of which the rhythm and melodic line offer a certain appearance of affinity with a phrase of César Franck's:

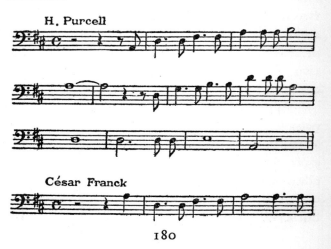

Purcell's phrase, which we have taken from the anthem *Praise the Lord, O Jerusalem,* is the setting of the words " Be thou exalted, Lord, in thine own strength " (Psalm xxi. 13). That of César Franck interprets the first verse of Psalm cl: " Praise ye the Lord. Praise God in His sanctuary: Praise Him in the firmament of His power (*Louez le Dieu caché dans ses saints tabernacles; Louez le Dieu qui règne en son immensité*)." How are we to explain the apparent kinship between these two phrases, except by the fact that a like aspiration of the soul may find expression in a lyrical flight of a similar nature even in two masters separated by an interval of two centuries?

We need hardly point out that there is a passage in one of Wagner's works which offers a striking analogy with the Fugue in B flat, and especially with the following passage from the ode of 1682 (P. S. Ed., XV, 45–4).

Richard Wagner knew England, and he cannot have been unacquainted with Purcell's work.

Die Meistersinger, more than any of his other works, shows how far he had assimilated the methods of composition of the old masters.

We would also call the attention of our readers to an article in the *Monde musical* for October 1925, in which M. André Mangeot proves, by means of examples, how great is the resemblance between the writing of Purcell's Fantasias and that of Gabriel Fauré's string quartet. "The harmonic treatment of Fauré's work," says Monsieur A. Mangeot, "shows us that his style of writing has profited by the musical evolution which has taken place since Purcell's day." But he goes on to say that "we may none the less note that his methods are exactly the same. Fauré's inspiration is slightly less varied than that of Purcell: we may recall the fact that Fauré wrote his first string quartet at the age of twenty-four, whereas Purcell was twenty-two when he composed his four-part Fantasias. For my own part, I am not surprised to see that, at the end of his long life, Fauré seems to have come to the conclusion that this is evidently the best way to write, while Purcell, two centuries and a half before him, had habitually written in this way, since in his day all musicians of culture were practised in contrapuntal writing. . . ." This return to an older style on the part of Fauré may perhaps show "that what we call progress is really no more than a process of change, and that both art and life revolve eternally in the same infinite cycle." Monsieur Mangeot considers that in his Fantasias "the great English composer touches the apogee of his achievement," and for our own part we would subscribe to this judgment. Not only the ear, but the eye too receives an impression of sheer beauty when confronted with the writing of the Fantasias.

"We may hope for sound criticism," we read in *L'Orgue et les organistes* (August 15, 1925), of which M. Jean Huré is the editor, "if only writers will refrain from hunting after musical reminiscences." But Monsieur Huré may be reassured as to the purity of our intentions. It would be fruitless, and consequently reprehensible, for us to hunt after these musical reminiscences if our object were to cast aspersions upon the fame of later masters who have consciously or unconsciously echoed Purcell. But our sole object is to show that the English musician belongs by right to the race of true geniuses, and that his works are a source upon which famous composers have not disdained to draw.

V

Tributes to Henry Purcell

We FEEL REAL SATISFACTION IN THE thought that the musicians of Purcell's day all bowed before his superior genius. There is an allusion to this fact in a fine ode written by Dryden after the master's death and set to music by John Blow, in which he says that, just as the lark and linnet cease to dispute the palm of song when, " in the close of night, . . . Philomel begins her heavenly lay ":

So ceased the rival crew, when Purcell came,
They sung no more, or only sung his fame:
    Struck dumb, they all admired
    The godlike man.
    Alas! too soon retired,
    As he too late began.

The highest of tributes was paid to the musician's memory when he received the honour of burial in Westminster Abbey itself; his body lies there close to the organ, with the following inscription:

Plaudite, felices Superi, tanto hospite; nostris
Præfuerat, vestris additur ille choris.
Invida nec vobis Purcellum terra reposcat,
Questa decus secli, deliciasque breves.
Tam cito decessisse, modos cui singula debet
Musa, prophana suos, religiosa suos!
Vivit, Io! et vivat, dum vicina organa spirant,
Dumque colet numeris turba canora Deum!

of which Dr. Cummings gives the following translation:

Applaud so great a guest, celestial pow'rs,
Who now resides with you, but once was ours.
Yet let invidious earth no more reclaim
Her short-lived fav'rite and her chiefest fame;
Complaining that so prematurely died

Good-nature's pleasure and devotion's pride.
Died? No, he lives, while yonder organs sound
And sacred echoes to the choir rebound.

A tablet has been placed upon a pillar close by his tombstone, on which may be read the following inscription:

Here lies Henry Purcell, Esq., who left this life, and is gone to that blessed place where only his harmony can be exceeded. Obiit 21mo die Novembris, anno ætatis suæ 37mo. Annoq. Domini 1695.

In 1706 the body of Mrs. Purcell was laid by that of her husband.

Daniel Purcell, who always continued to cherish the same affection and admiration for his elder brother, wrote a funeral ode in his memory, entitled " A Lamentation for the death of Mr. Henry Purcell," the words of which were written by Nahum Tate, and end as follows:

A sighing Wind, a murm'ring Rill
Our ears with doleful Accents fill:
They are heard, and only they,
For sadly thus they seem to say:
The Joy, the Pride of Spring is Dead,
The Soul of Harmony is fled.

Pleasure's flown from Albion's shore,
Wit and Mirth's bright Reign is o'er,
Strephon and music are no more!
Since Nature thus pays Tribute to his Urn,
How should a sad, forsaken Brother mourn!

Tudway wrote in reference to the anthem *Blessed is the Man,* sung at the funeral service for Queen Mary: " I appeal to all that were present, as well such as understood music as those that did not, whether they ever heard anything so rapturously fine and solemn, and so heavenly in the operation, which drew tears from all; and yet it is a plain, natural composition, which shows the power of music when rightly fitted and adapted to devotional purposes."

Henry Hall wrote an ode in memory of the master, of which the opening verses are as follows:

Hail! and for ever hail, harmonious Shade!
I loved thee living, and admire thee dead.
Apollo's harp at once our souls did strike;
We learnt together, but not learnt alike:
Though equal care our master might bestow,
Yet only Purcell's e'er shall equal Blow;
For thou by Heaven for wondrous things design'd
Left'st thy Companion lagging far behind.

Sometimes a Hero in an age appears,
But once a Purcell in a Thousand Years!

We may also mention a pastoral elegy entitled *Damon,* by J. Gilbert, of Christ's College, Cambridge, published by Heptinstall in 1696 on black-edged paper, in which there is a dialogue between Thyrsis and Damon. The latter utters a lament on the death of Purcell, and calls upon the Muses, the Graces, Venus, Cupid, the Dryads, Fauns, and Sylvans, and all Nature to share his grief. The style of this piece is somewhat artificial, but it has a note of true sincerity. We cannot refrain from quoting some quaint Latin verses written in the form of a rebus by Tomlinson, and set as a catch by Lenton, a member of King William III and Queen Mary's Music, which sings the praises of the musician's skill. The solution of the rebus is, of course: Hen-rye, Purr-cell.

> *Galli marita, par tritico seges,*
> *Prænomen est ejus dat chromati leges;*
> *Intrat cognomen blanditiis cati,*
> *Exit eremi in ædibus stati;*
> *Expertum effectum omnes admirentur.*
> *Quid merent Poetæ? Ut bene calcentur!*

The Mate to a Cock, and Corn tall as Wheat
Is his Christian Name, who is Musick's Compleat;

His Sirname begins with the Grace of a Cat,
And concludes with the House of a Hermit, note that;
His Skill and Performance each Auditor Wins,
But the Poet deserves a good kick on the Shins.

We might enumerate a long list of pane-
gyrics upon Purcell. We need only add that his
fame crossed the Channel. Many of his sonatas
were published at Amsterdam. Corelli had a high
opinion of him, and one of his biographers relates that he had intended to pay Purcell a visit,
and was deterred only by the news of the English master's death.

But it was not only the musician whom his
contemporaries loved in Purcell; it was the man
himself. At the beginning of the second volume
of the *Orpheus Britannicus* we read the following verses:

Make room, ye happy natures of the sky,
Room for a soul, all Love and Harmony;
A Soul that rose to such Perfection here,
It scarce will be advanced by being there.

And we read below:

Pride was the sole aversion of his Eye;
Himself was Humble as his Art was High.

Is not modesty one of the distinctive features
of truly noble natures? In the dedication of the

first collection of sonatas, addressed to Charles II, we have seen how Purcell attributes all his merit to the King's favour. The spirit of this dedication offers some analogy with that in which Bach, in presenting his *Six Concertos for several instruments* to the Margrave of Brandenburg, speaks of the " small talents " with which Heaven has endowed him.

Grabu, on the other hand, in dedicating *Albion and Albanius* to King James II, alludes to his own work in the following terms: " As the subject of this opera is naturally magnificent, it could not but excite my genius and raise it to a greater height in the composition — even so as to surpass itself." Comment is superfluous.

We may, however, point out that on one occasion Purcell had to suffer for his easy-going reputation. The publishers J. May and J. Hudgebutt, having been so fortunate as to obtain possession of the score of *The Indian Queen,* published it without the composer's sanction. To justify this act of piracy they pleaded that the composer's modesty was so great that it was only with extreme difficulty that he could be persuaded to " patronize " his own works, and they had been afraid lest an imperfect copy of his admirable songs might be placed in the hands of the public. They had, however, no doubt that his candour and generosity would induce him to excuse their presumption. Purcell does not seem to have been perturbed at this dishonesty on the part of the publishers.

We may conclude this section of our work with a panegyric on the master, composed by a man who had protested against the immorality of the age, and used hard words about both poets and musicians: the Rev. Arthur Bedford, chaplain to the Duke of Bedford and Vicar of the Temple, Bristol. " Our Purcell," he says, " was the delight of the nation and the wonder of the world." These words may be found in his work entitled *On the Evil and Danger of Stage Plays*.

Many French writers on music have done justice to Henry Purcell. The first, perhaps, to draw attention to his merits and speak of his genius was Amédée Méreaux, celebrated in his day both as a pianist and as an art-critic, in his *Les Clavecinistes de 1637 à 1790* (1867).

The death of Purcell was a terrible blow to British music, which was now submerged by the rising tide of Italian music. John Blow died, disheartened, in 1708. In 1727, with the object of producing a reaction against foreign influence, John Gay produced his *Beggar's Opera*. Under the pretext of scourging the vices of receivers of stolen property, highwaymen, and pickpockets he arraigned the courtiers and politicians of the day and railed at his contemporaries for being so infatuated with Italian opera. In order to rally the English public to the cause of national art he presented them with a nosegay of old ballads, in the desire to bring home to them the fragrance of their national folk-lore. And, indeed, British folk-lore is incomparably rich.

But soon Handel reigned supreme in the artistic world, without, however, founding a school in the strict sense of the word.

In the nineteenth century Mendelssohn aroused the admiration of England by his oratorios, and especially by the *Elijah,* the purity and nobility of which are universally appreciated in that country — as is, indeed, only just. The influence of Mendelssohn was considerable. At a later date Brahms was also in great vogue for a time.

For the last fifty years England has been recovering her position, and we are witnessing a regular renaissance of British music, drawing its inspiration from national sources. What is more, it cannot be too often repeated that there is scarcely another country in which choirs of more imposing volume are to be found than in Great Britain, in which public halls are better arranged for listening to music, or in which organs are more numerous or more carefully tended, as M. Louis Vierne notes, in *L'Orgue et les organistes* for May 15, 1924.

Great Britain has produced admirable painters. Reynolds, Gainsborough, Opie, Constable, Bonington, Turner, Madox Brown, Dante Gabriel Rossetti, Burne-Jones, Watts, Alfred Parsons, Poynter, and others have justly achieved fame, whether in portraiture, in landscape, or in the historical or symbolical style, and have enriched the artistic heritage of humanity. But did the pictorial art spring up and flourish in Great Britain as naturally and spontaneously as that of music? Our answer to this question is in the negative. The English sovereigns of former days summoned to their court famous foreign artists. Mabuse, Johannes Corvus, Lucas Cornelis, Holbein, Antonio Moro, Rubens, Van Dyck, among others, lived or settled in England, long before the pictorial art in England had become fully conscious of its powers. The works that they left behind them contributed in no small measure to its development and magnificent bloom. In encouraging music, as we said at the beginning of this work, these sovereigns did not attempt to impose their own taste on their subjects. It was rather the taste of the people that imposed itself on the sovereigns, or, at any rate, in following the cult of music the tastes of both were in harmony. When King Charles II welcomed to his court musicians from France, Germany, and Italy, England had already seen the rise of great composers, and the art of music had been honoured for centuries past. To sum up, this devotion to music was the fruit of a deeply rooted national tendency.

None the less, it cannot be denied that, owing to the effect of foreign influences, English music lost consciousness of itself during the eighteenth and early nineteenth centuries. Not that it did so entirely. The flood of foreign influences failed completely to extinguish the fires of art that had been kindled by earlier generations. There were a number of composers during this period. They did not lack technical skill, but none of them was inspired by the breath of genius. No composer of religious music had the fervour of William Byrd or Orlando Gibbons; in the dramatic style, none possessed Purcell's lyrical gifts; none had the popular charm of Weelkes or the gift of expressing his own emotions adequately. The style in which these composers wrote is correct, but lacking in boldness; their rhythms had no variety; in a word, their art is devoid of originality. They made an honest attempt to keep their art alive when it was threatened with total extinction after the soul of Purcell had departed. But their powers were not commensurate with their conscientiousness. All the same, the part that they played was not utterly sterile; they were preparing for the revival that we are witnessing today.

It is the memory or the vague consciousness of this century and a half, during which the lamp of music in England burnt with such a feeble gleam and diffused such a faint influence, that causes English music to be judged so unfavourably, and, we may say, so unjustly, on the Continent. People forget — or are perhaps ignorant — that for nearly two centuries before the Puritan revolution, there had been centres of art in that country which had glowed with a most brilliant radiance. If, as we remarked at the opening of this study, the Restoration period may be regarded as the golden age of English music, this is because, under the influence of a prince who was a lover of the arts, these scattered lights were concentrated in one great flame of extraordinary intensity, in which furnace was forged the genius of Henry Purcell, who, while respecting the teaching of the old polyphonic school, was none the less one of the creators of modern music; Purcell, the ornament, not only of his age, but also of his country; Purcell, whose work, with its marvellous variety, is one of the rarest jewels in the poetic treasury of Great Britain; Purcell, in short, whose name has been handed down through the ages, and will always be so handed down, because he knew how to express human feeling in a language all divine.

APPENDIX

LIST *of* DRAMATIC WORKS

FOR WHICH PURCELL COMPOSED THE MUSIC,
WITH APPROXIMATE DATES
OF COMPOSITION

1695. *Abdelazer* (Mrs. Aphra Behn).

1690. *Amphitryon* (John Dryden).

 ? . *Aurengzebe* (John Dryden).

1695. *Bonduca* (anonymous adaptation from Beaumont
and Fletcher).

1695. *The Canterbury Guests* (E. Ravenscroft).

1685. *Circe* (Charles Davenant).

1692. *Cleomenes* (Dryden and Lee).

1689. *Dido and Æneas* (Nahum Tate).

1690. *Dioclesian* (adapted by Betterton from *The Prophetess*, by Beaumont and Fletcher).

1690. *Distressed Innocence* (E. Settle).

1694. *Don Quixote* Pt. I   (Tom d'Urfey).

1694.   —   Pt. II (—   ).

1695.   —   Pt. III (—   ).

1693. *The Double Dealer* (Congreve).

1682? 1685? *The Double Marriage* (Beaumont and Fletcher).

1683? 1684? *The English Lawyer* (E. Ravenscroft).

1693. *Epsom Wells* (Shadwell).

1692. *The Fairy Queen* (anonymous adaptation of Shakspere's *Midsummer Night's Dream*).

1694. *The Fatal Marriage* (Southerne).

1688. *A Fool's Preferment* (Beaumont and Fletcher, adapted by Tom d'Urfey).

1693. *The Female Vertuosos* (Thomas Wright).

1691. *The Gordian Knot Untyed* (author unknown).

1692. *Henry the Second* (Bancroft?).

1691. *The Indian Emperor* (Dryden).

1695. *The Indian Queen* (Sir Robert Howard).

1691. *King Arthur* (Dryden).

1681. *King Richard the Second* (adapted from Shakspere by Nahum Tate).

1686? *The Knight of Malta* (adapted from Beaumont and Fletcher).

1692? 1695? *The Libertine* (Shadwell).

1694. *Love Triumphant* (Dryden).

1693. *The Maid's Last Prayer* (Southerne).

1692. *The Marriage Hater Matched* (T. d'Urfey).

1694. *The Married Beau* (Crowne).

1690. *The Massacre of Paris* (N. Lee).

1695. *The Mock Marriage* (Thomas Scott).

1692? *Œdipus* (Dryden and Lee).

1693. *The Old Bachelor* (Congreve).

1695. *Oroonoko* (Southerne, founded on a story by Mrs. A. Behn).

1690. *Pausan as* (Norton).

1692. *Regulus* (Crowne).

1693. *The Richmond Heiress* (Tom d'Urfey).

1695. *The Rival Sisters* (Robert Gould).

1693. *Rule a Wife and Have a Wife* (John Fletcher).

1690. *Sir Anthony Love* (Southerne).

1681. *Sir Barnaby Whigg* (Tom d'Urfey).

1685? *Sophonisba* (N. Lee).

1694? 1695? *The Spanish Friar* (Dryden).

1695. *The Tempest* (Shakspere, adapted by T. Shadwell).

1680. *Theodosius* (N. Lee).

1694. *Timon of Athens* (T. Shadwell).

1694? 1695? *Tyrannic Love* (Dryden).

Thy word is a lantern.

Turn Thee again, O Lord, God of Hosts.

Turn Thou us. O good Lord.

Unto Thee will I cry.

We sing to Him whose wisdom.

Who hath believed our report?

Why do the heathen?

Beati omnes qui timent Dominum, Gloria Patri (in E flat).

Collection of Canons, Laudate Dominum, Gloria Patri, Alleluia.

Etc.

———————

BIBLIOGRAPHY

ARUNDELL, DENNIS D.: *Henry Purcell* (The World's Manuals, Oxford University Press, 1927).

BUCHMAYER, RICHARD: in *Sammelbände der Internationalen Musikgesellschaft*, 1900–1.

CŒURY, ANDRÉ: *Musique et littérature* (Paris, Bloud et Gay).

COLLES, H. C.: article on Purcell in Grove's *Dictionary of Music* (revised edition).

CUMMINGS, WILLIAM H.: *Purcell* (Great Musicians series, London, 1881).

DUSSAUZE, HENRI: *Captain Cooke and his Choir Boys* (Sorbonne thesis, Paris).

EMMANUEL, MAURICE: *Histoire de la langue musicale*. Vol. II, "*Les Intervalles. Les Échelles*" (Paris, Henri Laurens, 1911).

Encyclopédie de la musique (Paris, Delagrave).

FULLER-MAITLAND, J. A.: in *The Oxford History of Music*.

GÖHLINGER, FR. A.: *Geschichte des Klavichords*.

GROVE, SIR GEORGE: *Dictionary of Music and Musicians*.

KREBS, CARL: *Die besaiteten Klavierinstrumente bis zum Anfang des 17 Jahrhunderts*.

LANDORMY, PAUL: *Historie de la musique* (Paris, Delaplane-Mellotee).

PARRY, SIR HUBERT: in *The Oxford History of Music*.

RAUGEL, FÉLIX: *Les Organistes* (Paris, Laurens).

REYHER, PAUL: *Les Masques anglais* (Paris, Hachette).

RIEMANN, HUGO: *Musik-Lexicon* (Leipzig).

ROLLAND, ROMAIN: *Histoire de l'opéra en Europe avant Lully et Scarlatti* (Paris, Fontemoing).

—: *Musiciens d'autrefois* (Paris, Hachette) (English translation, *Some Musicians of Former Days* (London, Curwen; New York, Holt).

RUNCIMAN, JOHN F.: *Purcell* (Bell's Miniature Series of Musicians, London, 1909).

SQUIRE, WILLIAM BARCLAY: in *Sammelbände der Internationalen Musikgesellschaft*, Vols. V and VI.

WALKER, ERNEST: *A History of Music in England* (Oxford, Clarendon Press).

Readers are also referred to the articles by J. A. FULLER-MAITLAND in the *Dictionary of National Biography;* to the articles on musical instruments in the *Encyclopædia Britannica*, eleventh edition; and to other general works. See also H. CART DE LAFONTAINE: *The King's Musick, a transcript of records relating to music and musicians* (*1460–1700*) (1909); PIERRE LASSERE: *The Spirit of French Music* (1921); and the monographs: P. A. SCHOLES: *In Purcell's Time* (1913, No. 2 of the Music Student Handbooks); and W. BARCLAY SQUIRE: *Purcell's Dramatic Music* (1904).

For English music in general, see, in addition to the general histories of music: E. H. FELLOWES: *The English Madrigal* (The World's Manuals, Oxford University Press), and *The English Madrigal Composers* (Oxford University Press, 1921); PETER WARLOCK: *The English Ayre* (The World's Manuals, Oxford University Press); C. VON DER BORREN: *Sources of Keyboard Music in England* (1913); E. W. NAYLOR: *Shakespeare and Music* (Dent's Temple Shakespeare Manuals), *Shakespeare Music* (with illustrations of Elizabethan music), and *An Elizabethan Virginal Book* (with musical illustrations and a facsimile from the Fitzwilliam Virginal Book).

For the social life of the Tudor and Stuart periods, see: the diaries of Pepys and Evelyn; Traill: *Social England, Shakespeare's England* (2 vols., 1916); ALLARDYCE NICOLL: *The Development of the Theatre* (1927) and *British Drama* (1925); and ELIZABETH GODFREY: *Home Life under the Stuarts* (1925) and *Social Life under the Stuarts* (1904).

INDEX

INDEX

iii

iv

INDEX

A NOTE ON THE TYPE

in which this book is set

This book is set on the Linotype in Garamont, a modern rendering of the type first cut by Claude Garamont (1510–1561). He was a pupil of Geofroy Tory and is believed to have based his letters on the Venetian models. He gave to his letters a certain elegance and a feeling of movement which won for their creator an immediate reputation and the patronage of the French King, Francis I.

SET UP, ELECTROTYPED,
PRINTED AND BOUND BY THE PLIMPTON PRESS,
NORWOOD, MASS.
PAPER MANUFACTURED BY
S. D. WARREN CO.,
BOSTON

DATE DUE